Mom's Quiet Time Journal with Coloring Pages

Embracing Destiny
http://embracingdestinyblog.com

This journal belongs to:

Date:

My word of the year:

My favorite Bible verse:

Let us not become weary in doing good, for at the proper time we will reap a harvest if we do not give up.

~ Galatians 6:9

Date:

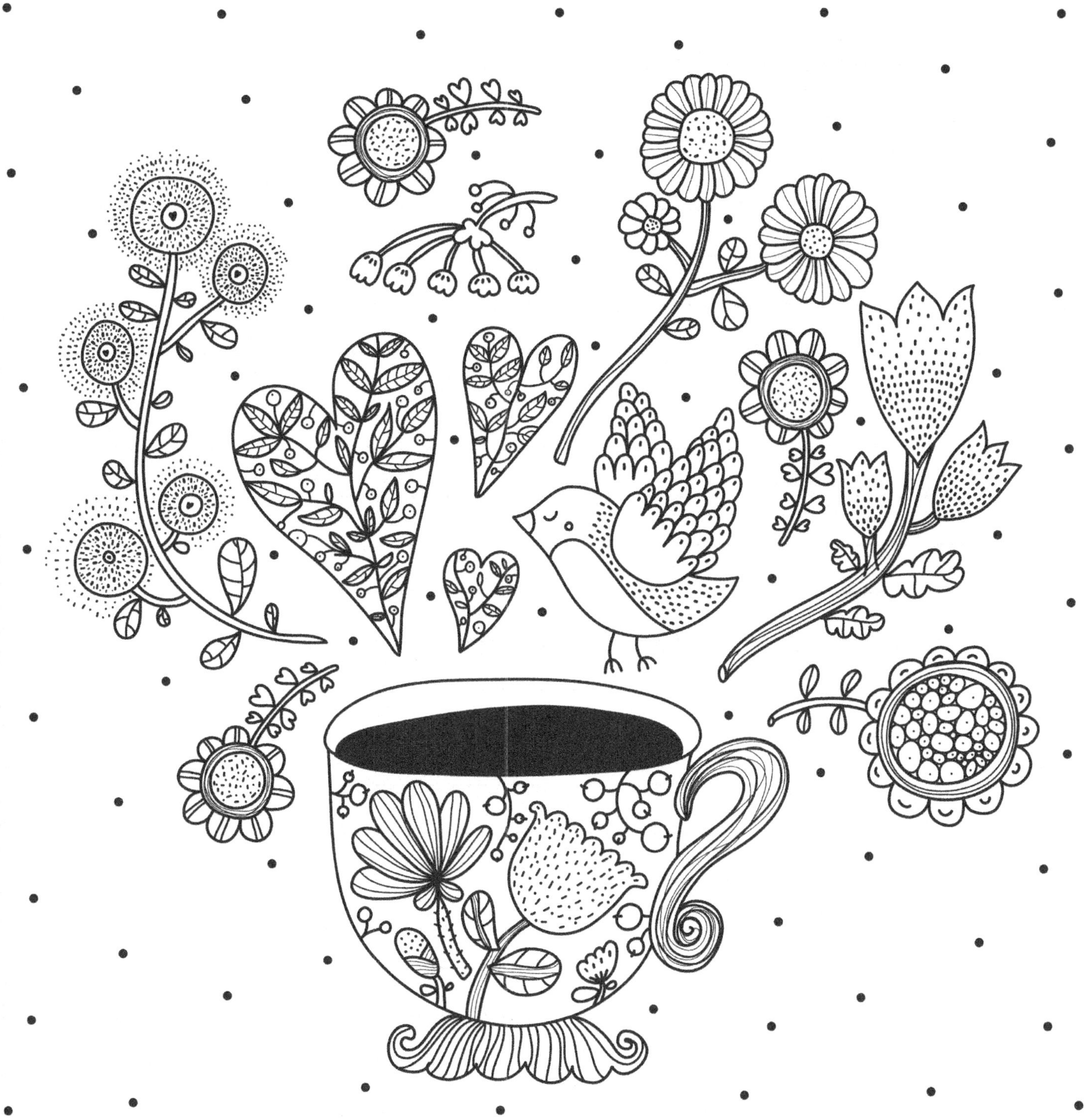

Time for a cuppa!

Date:

So Many Books, So Little Time!

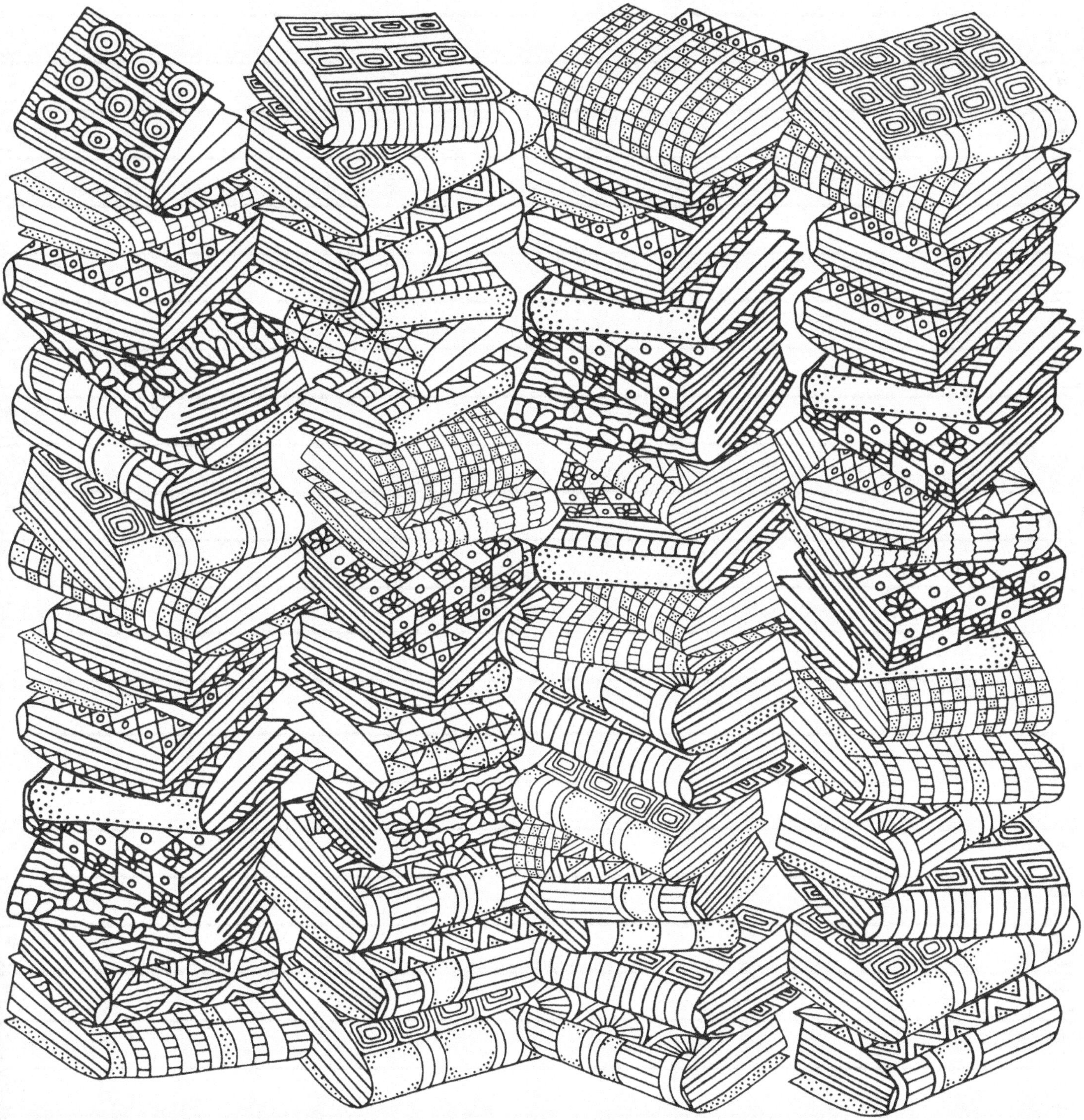

Books, Books, Books

Right now I'm reading:

What I want to read next:

Books, Books, Books

Right now I'm reading:

What I want to read next:

Moments I Want to Remember

Date:

Moments I Want to Remember

Date:

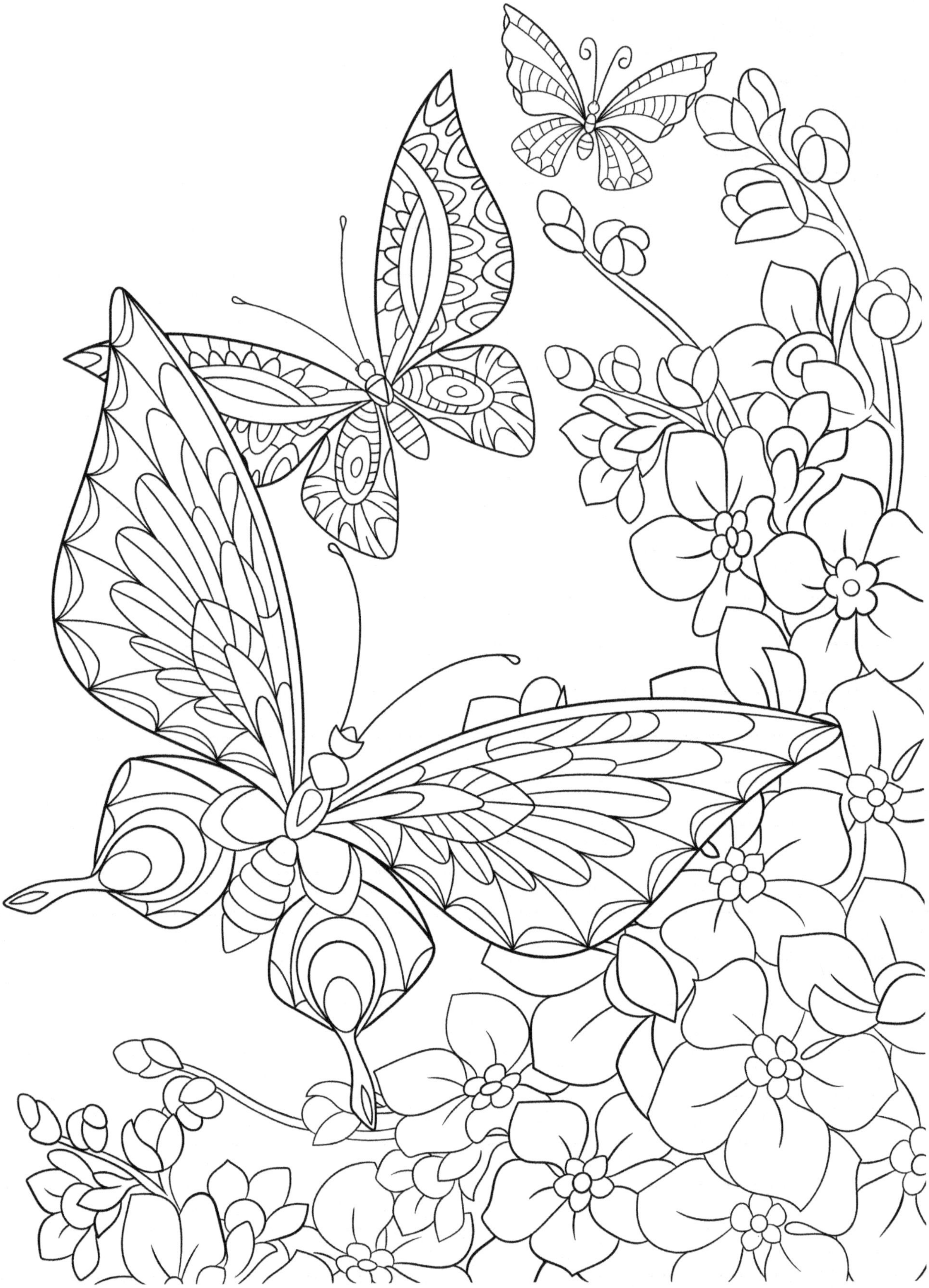

I'm Thankful For:

Date:

I'm Thankful For:

Date:

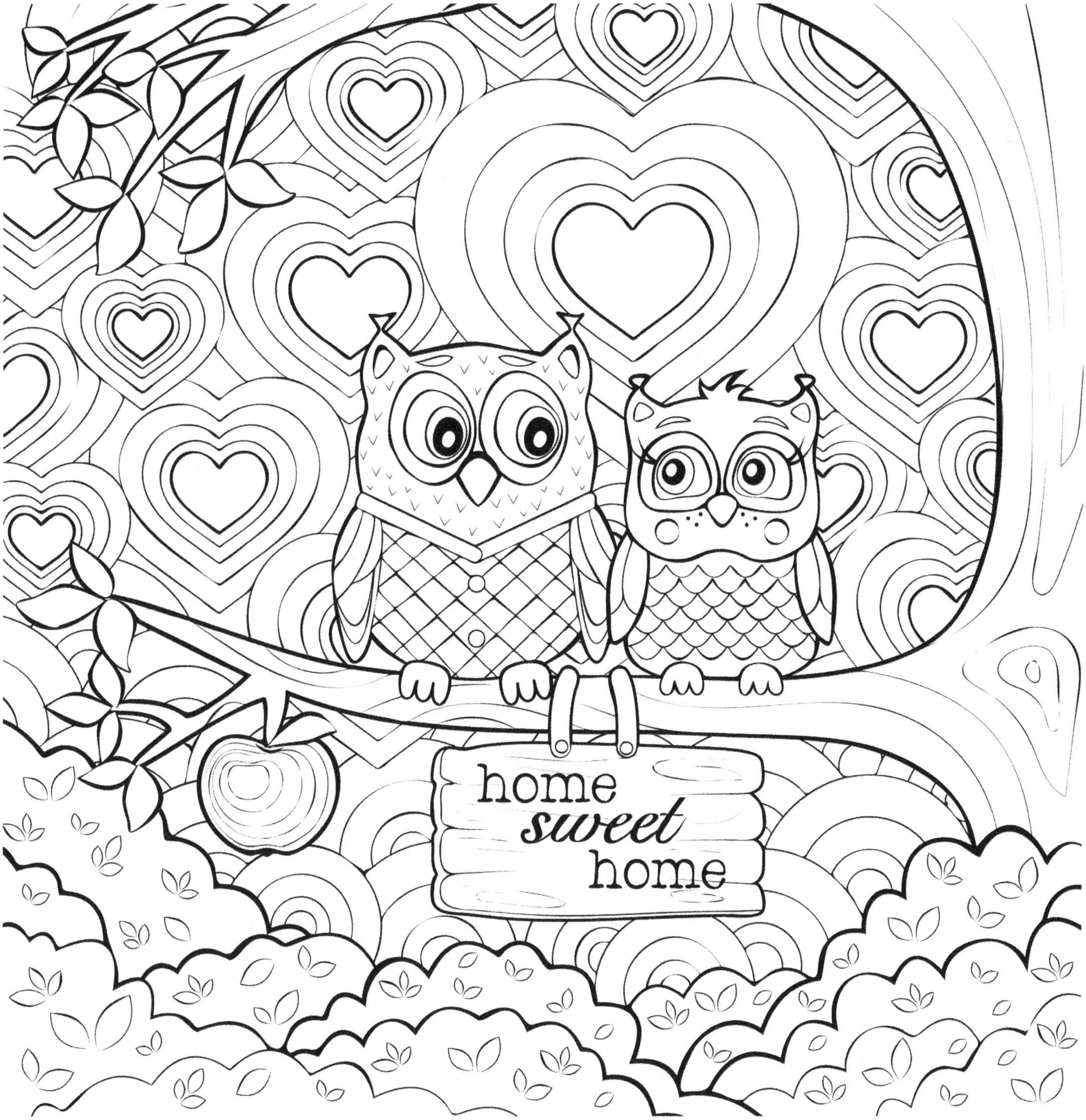
home
sweet
home

My Prayer List

Date: 5/20/24

- Jay & Tristen pregnancy - healthy baby/mom
- Hubby and kids
- Nana & my parents
- My Tia

My Prayer List

Date:

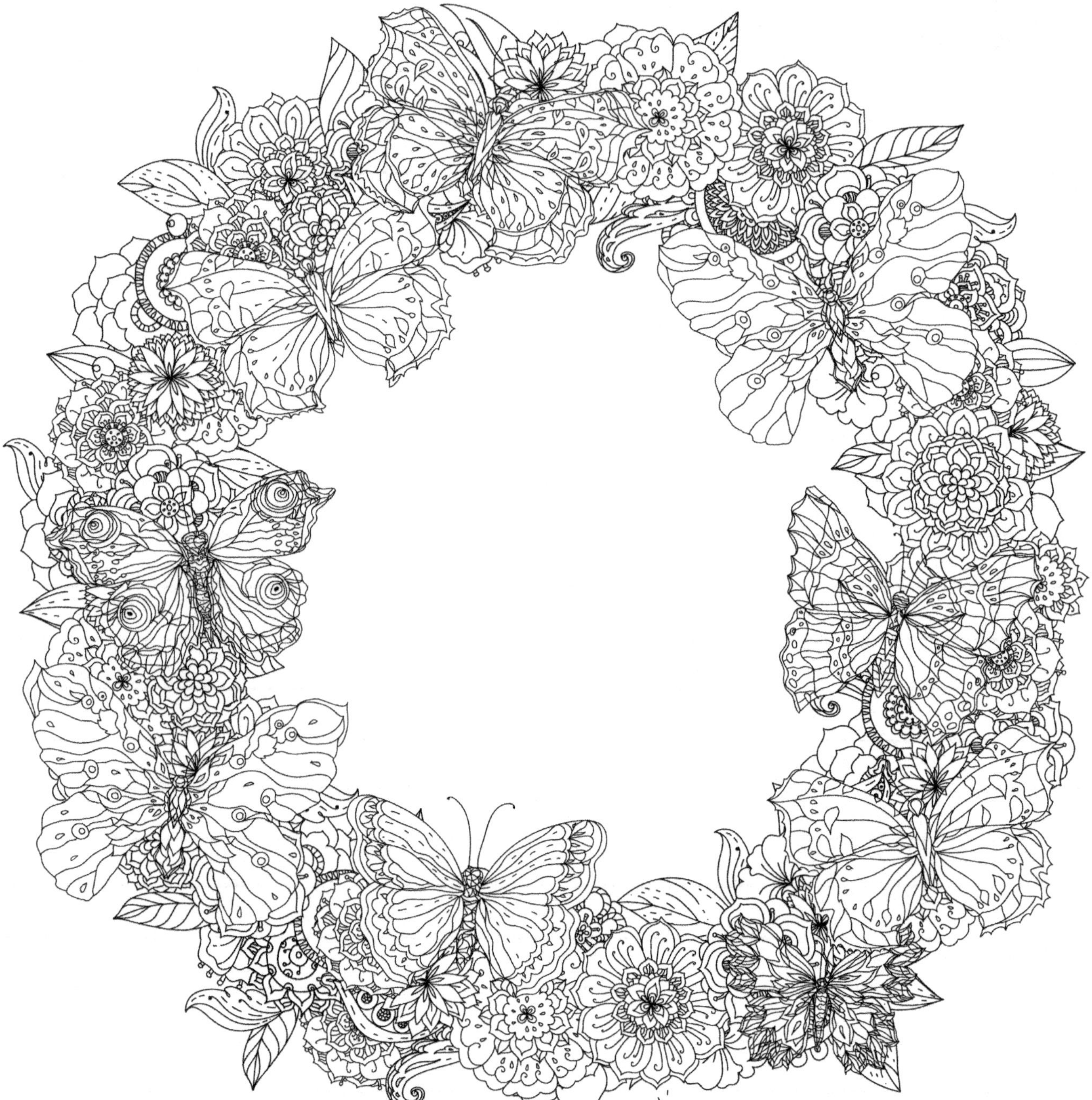

Bible Verses to Memorize:

Bible Verses to Memorize:

GARDEN

Places to Go:

Projects to Make:

Date:

Date:

Date:

Long-term Goals

Date:

Short-term Goals

Favorite Quotes and Inspiring Words to Live By

Favorite Quotes and Inspiring Words to Live By

The ordinary acts we practice every day at home are of more importance to the soul than their simplicity might suggest.

~ Thomas Moore

Date:

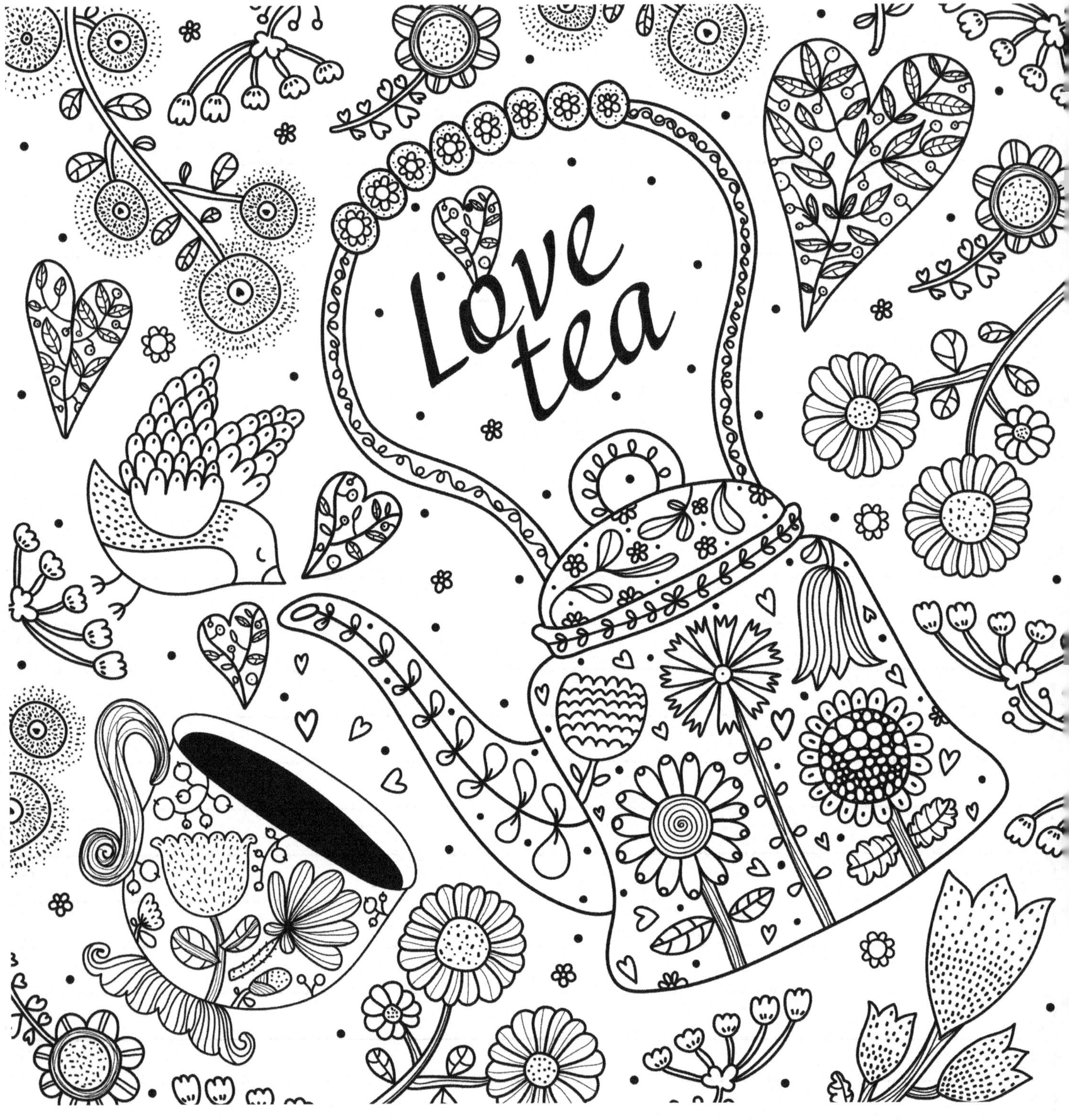
Love tea

Her children arise and call her blessed; her husband also, and he praises her.
~ Proverbs 31:28

Date:

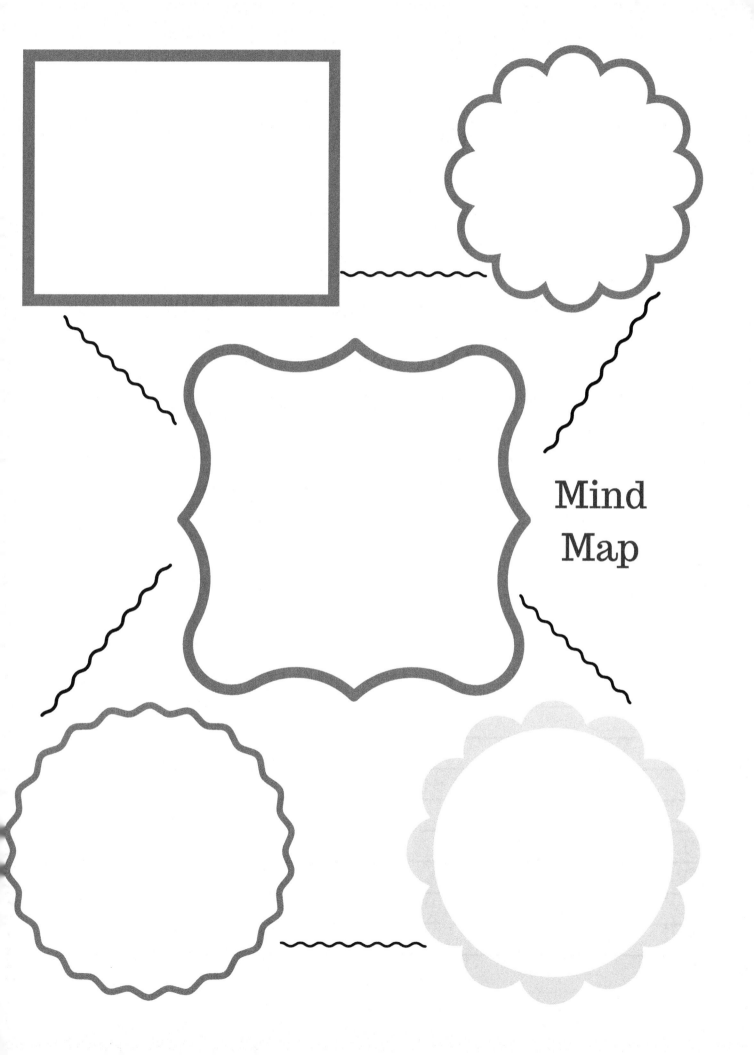

Mind
Map

Date:

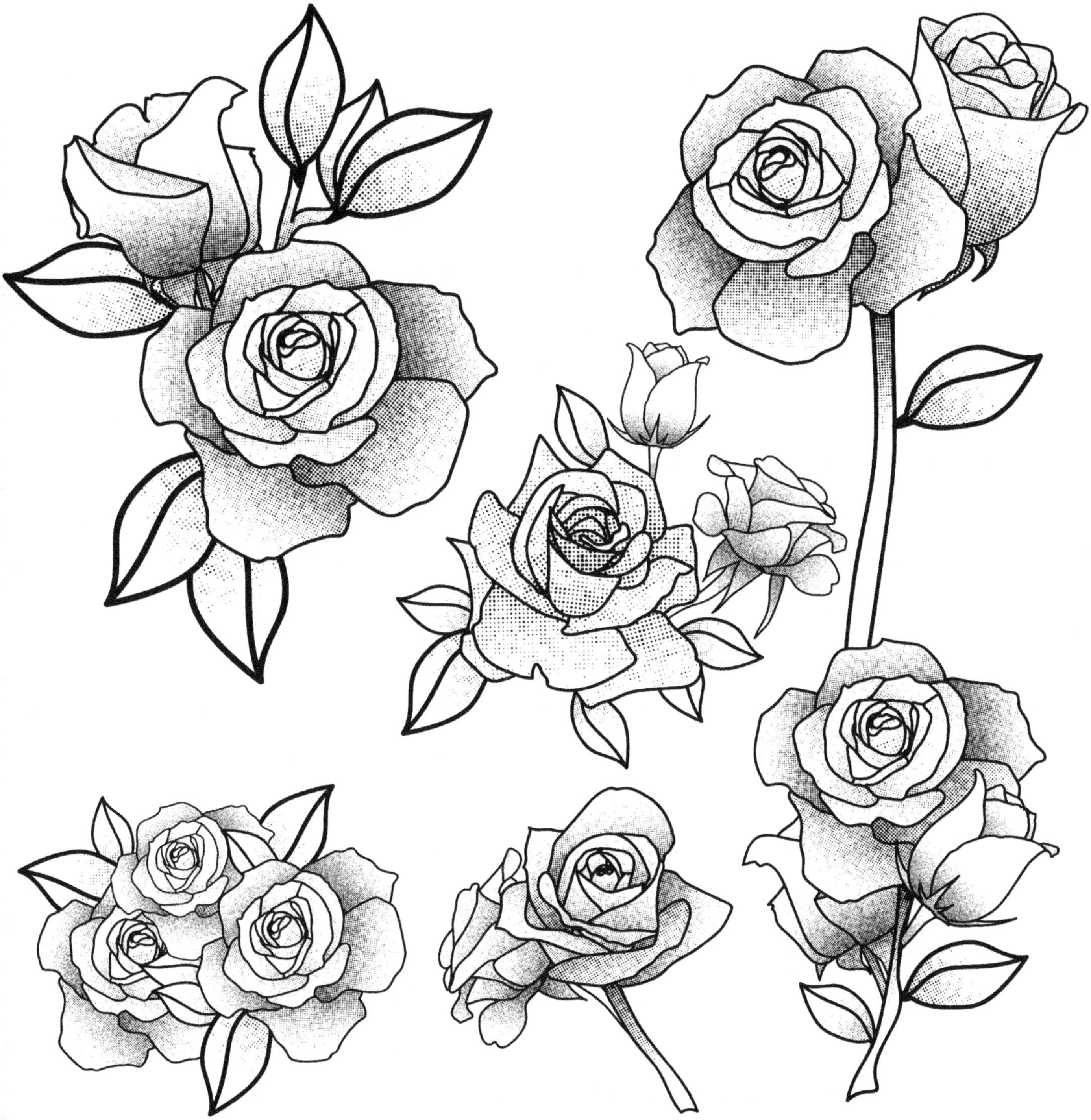

Date:

Date:

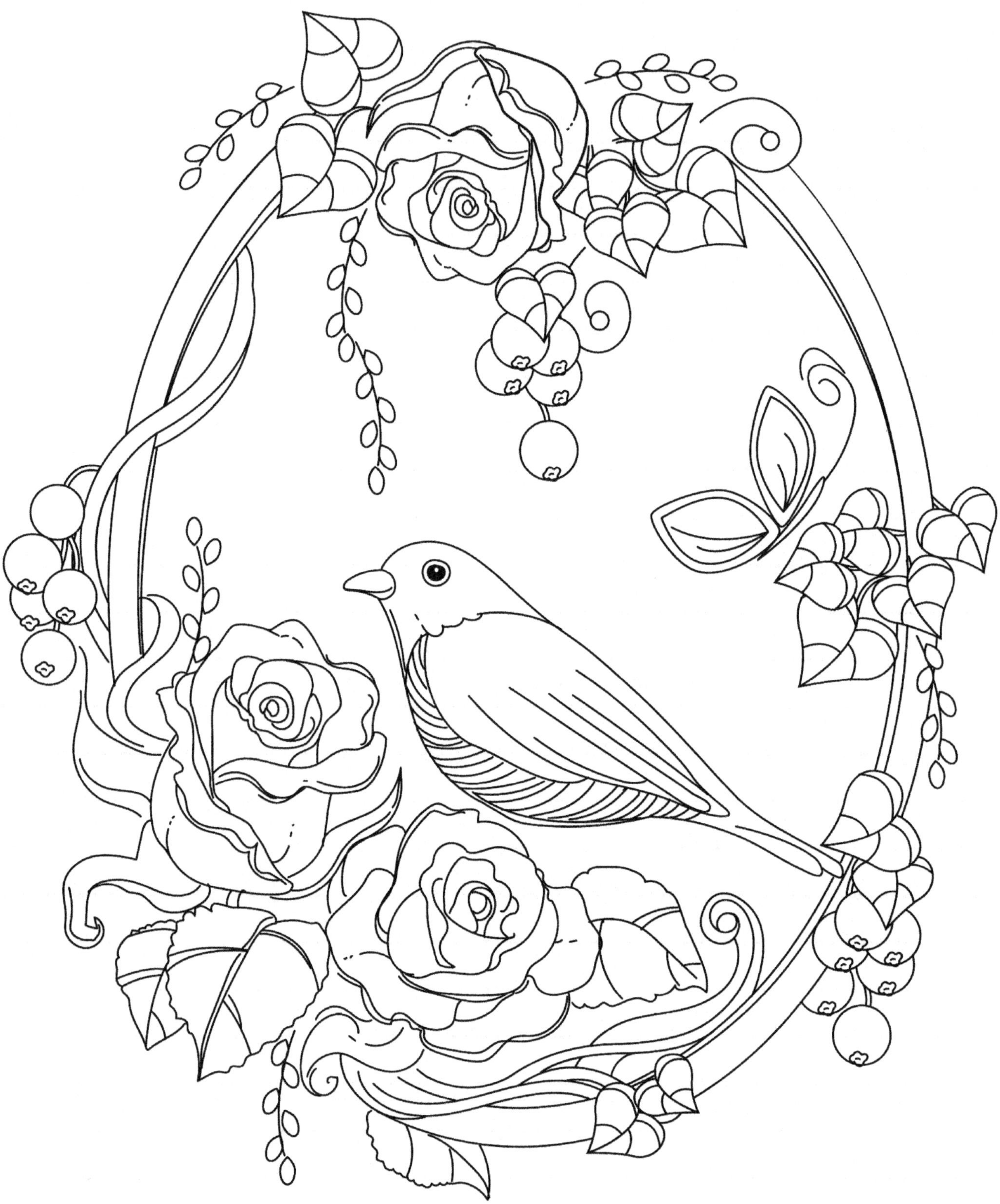

Date:

Date:

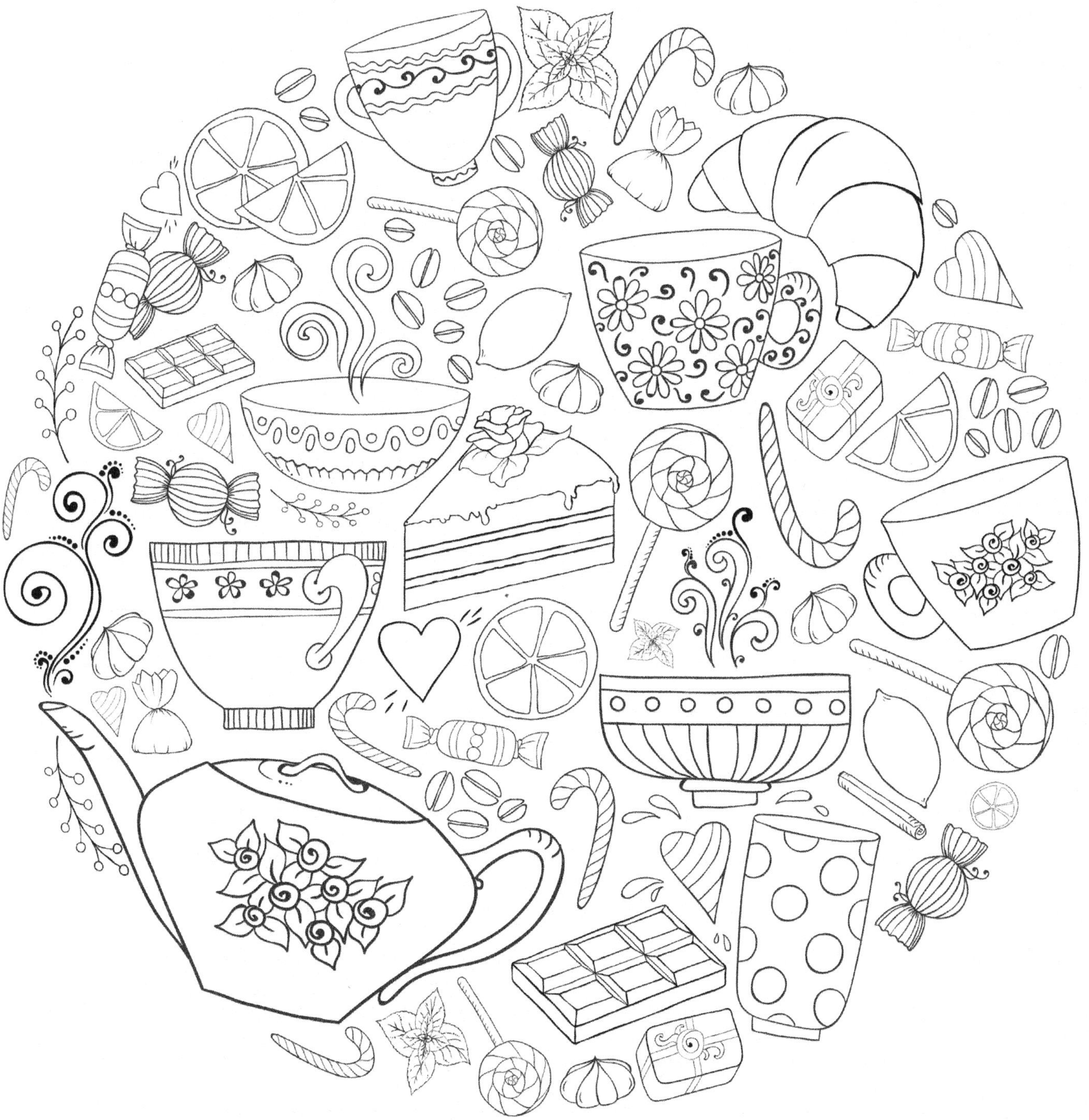

Date:

 Date:

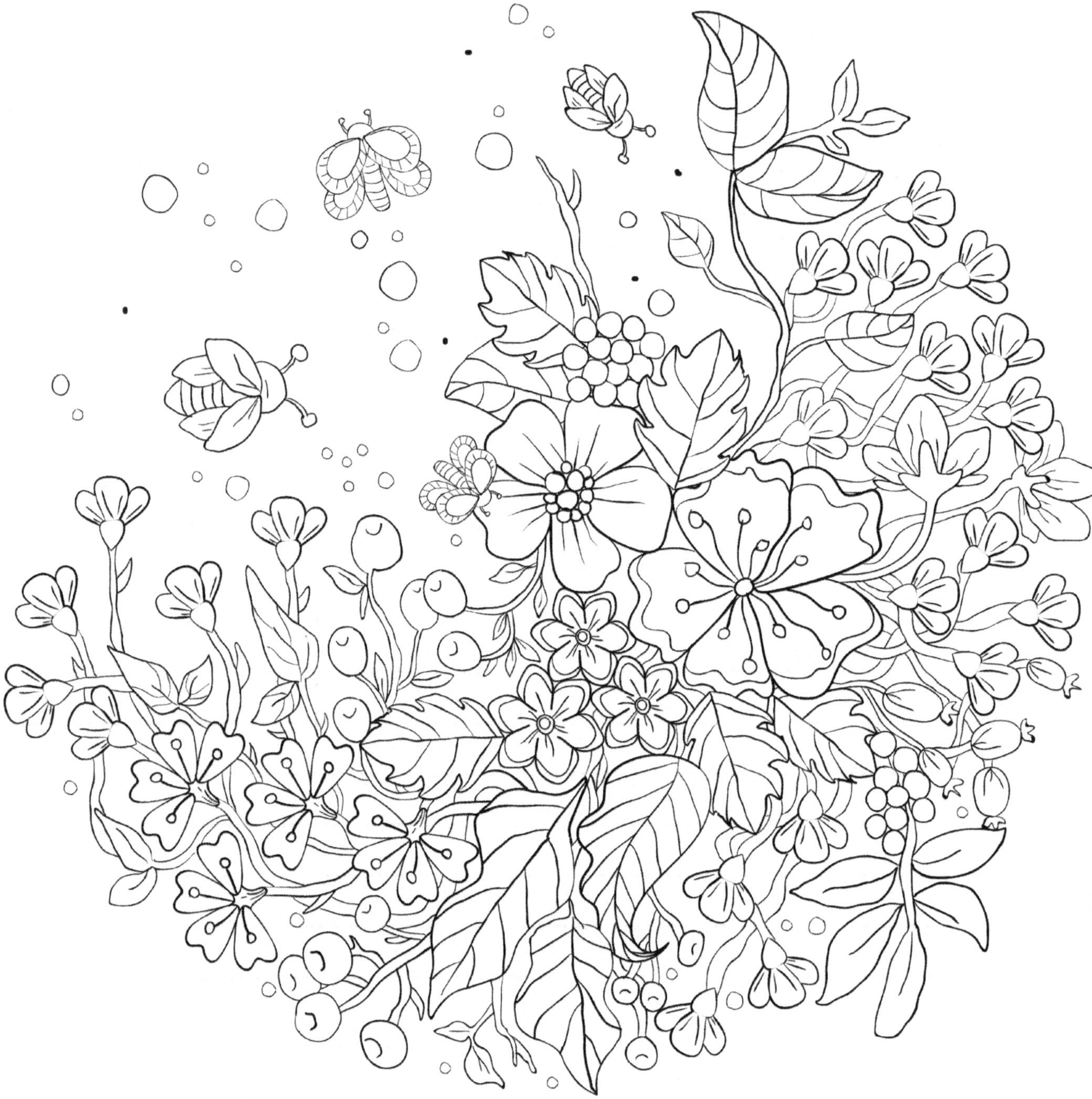

Consider the lilies, how they grow: they neither toil nor spin; but I tell you, no
even Solomon in all his glory clothed himself like one of these.
~Luke 12:27

Date:

Date:

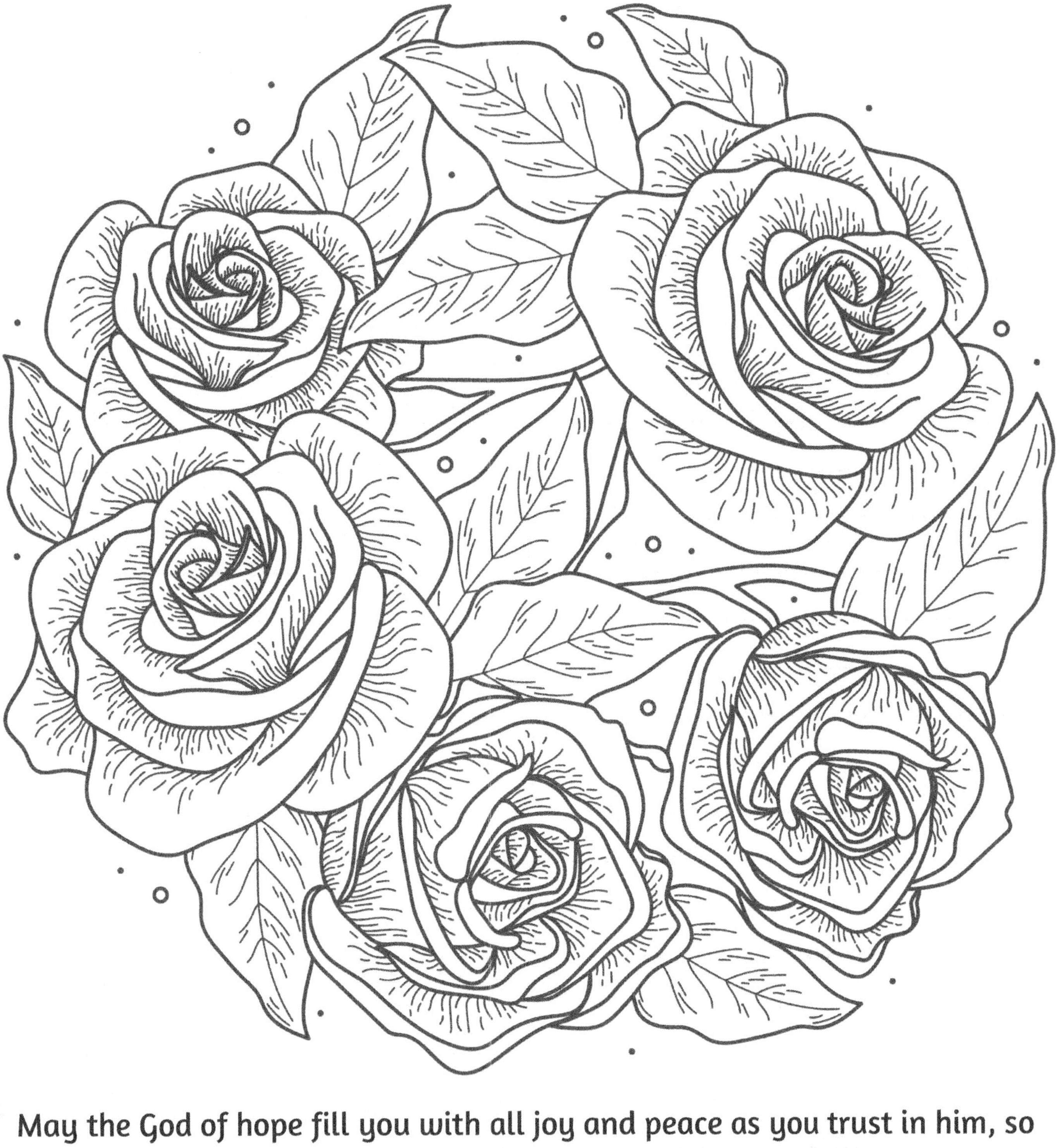

May the God of hope fill you with all joy and peace as you trust in him, so that you may overflow with hope by the power of the Holy Spirit.

~Romans 15:13

Date:

Date:

Date:

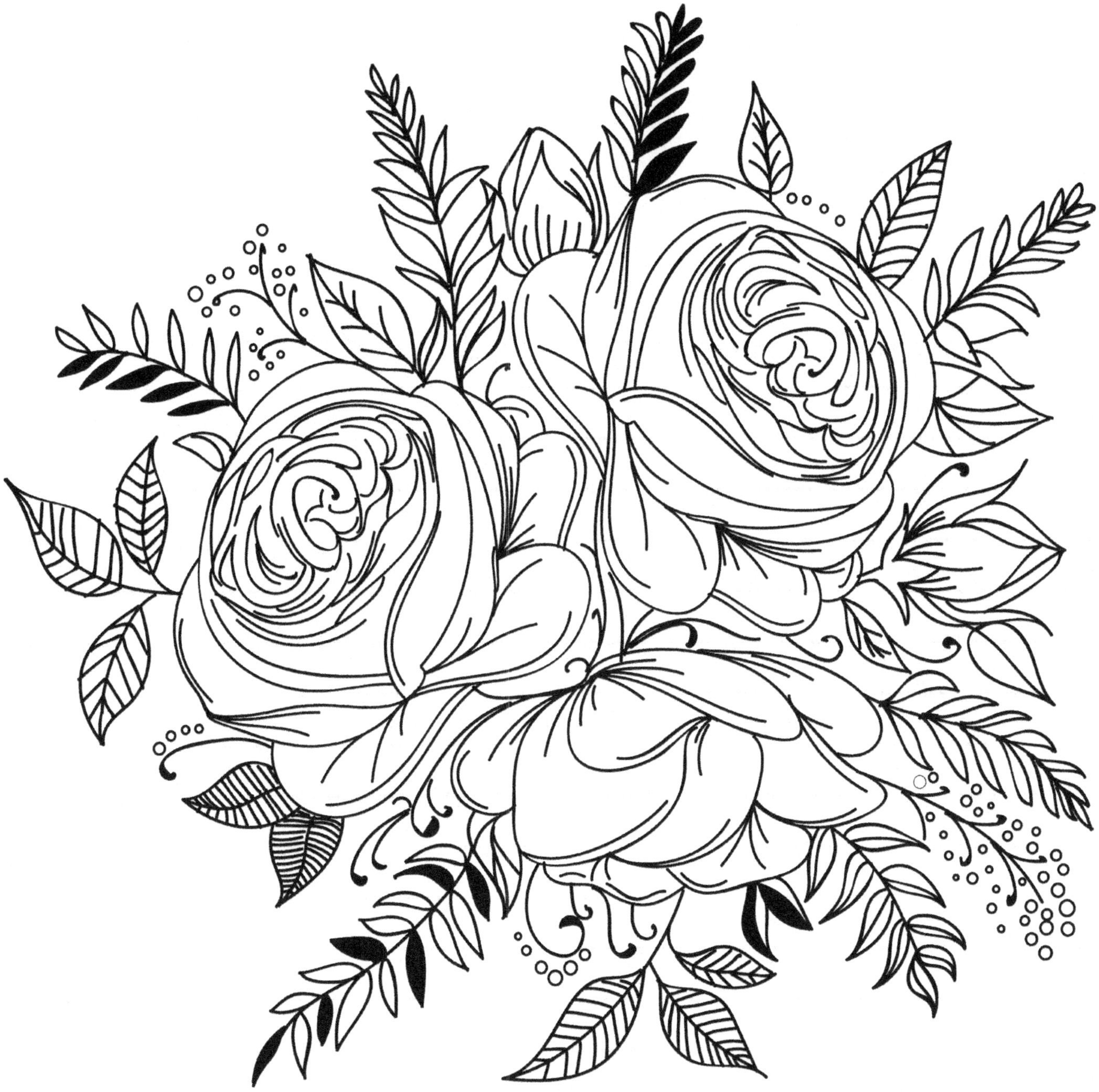

"Be still, and know that I am God;
I will be exalted among the nations,
I will be exalted in the earth."
~Psalm 46:10

Favorite Quotes and Inspiring Words to Live By

Favorite Quotes and Inspiring Words to Live By

Now faith is confidence in what we hope for and assurance about what we do not see.

~Hebrews 11:1

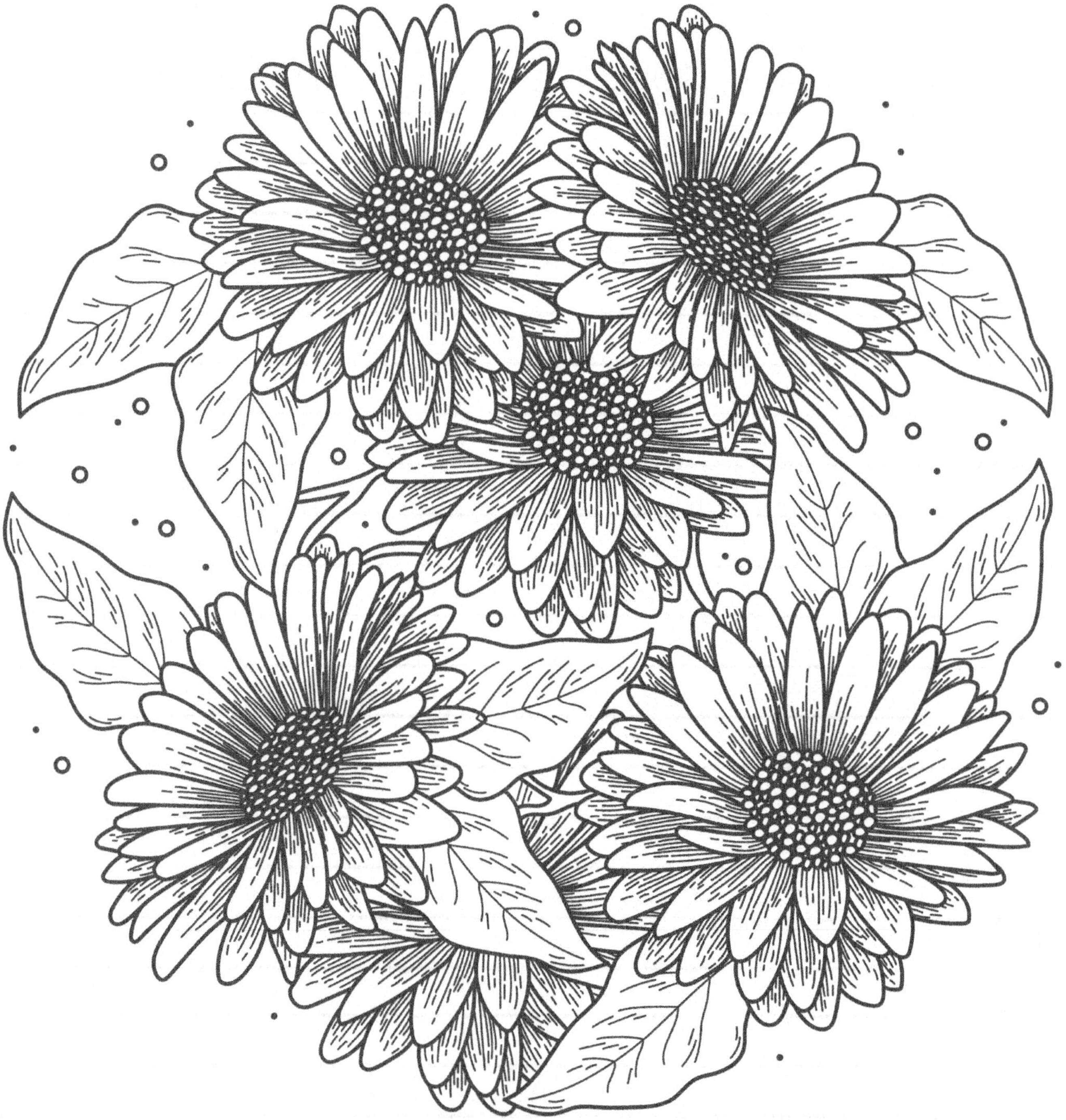

Favorite Quotes and Inspiring Words to Live By

Favorite Quotes and Inspiring Words to Live By

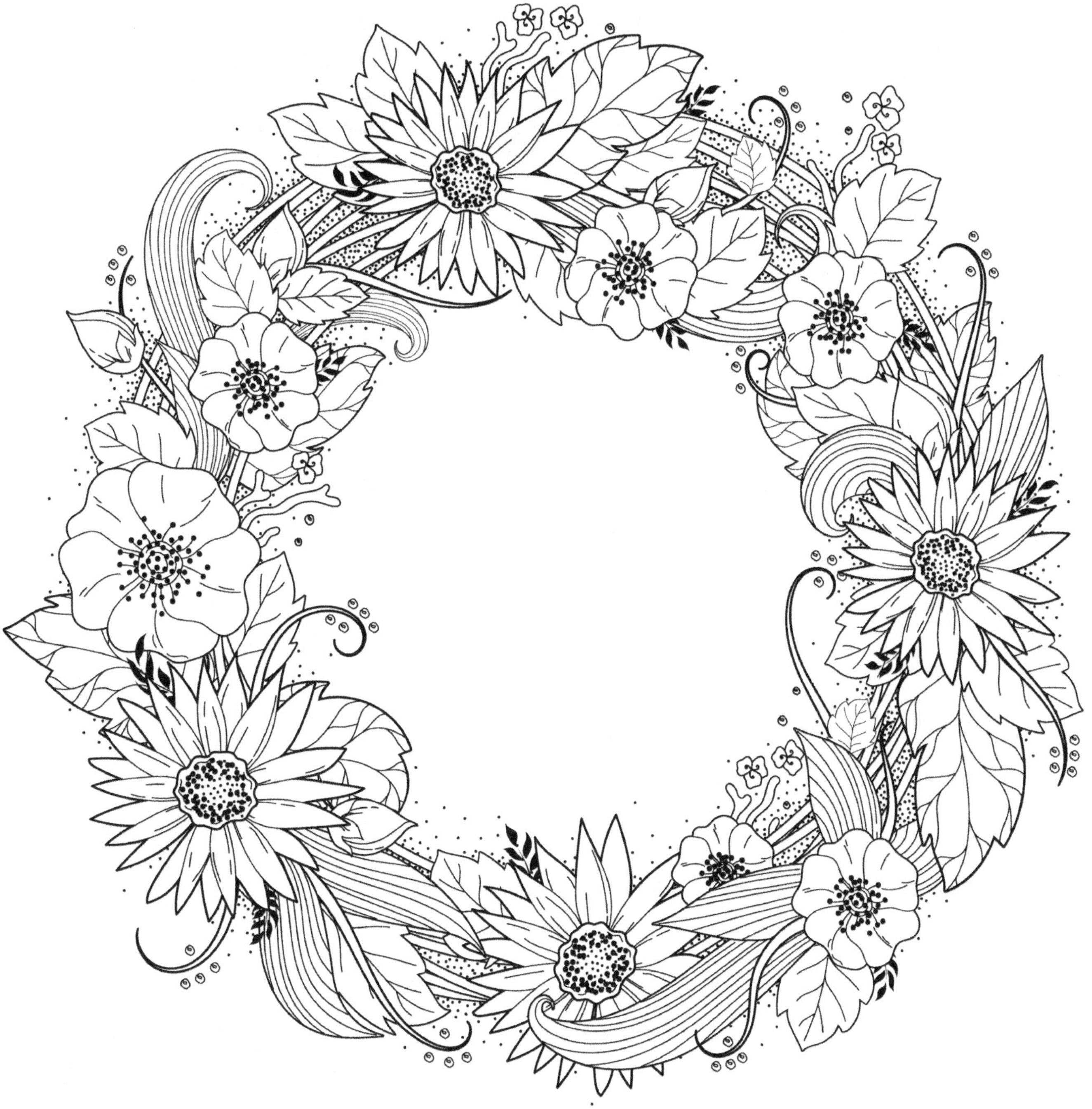

For I know the plans I have for you. declares the Lord, plans to prosper you and not to harm you, plans to give you hope and a future.

– Jeremiah 29:11

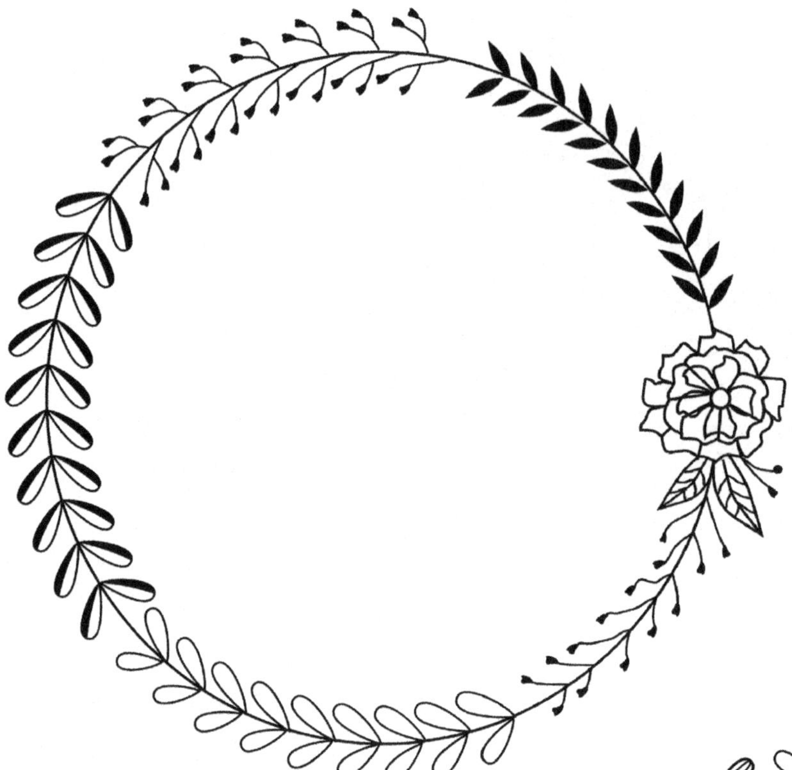

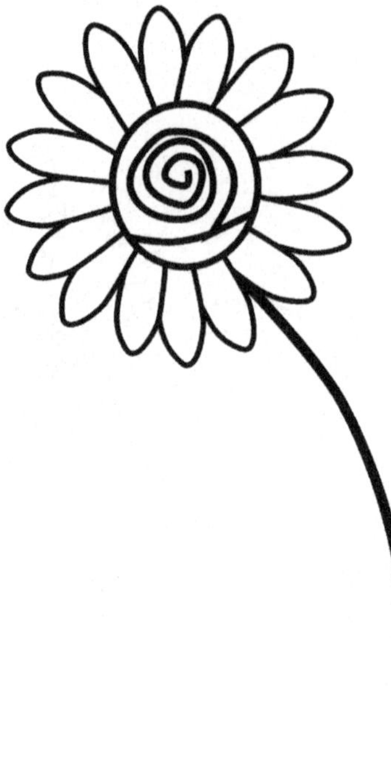

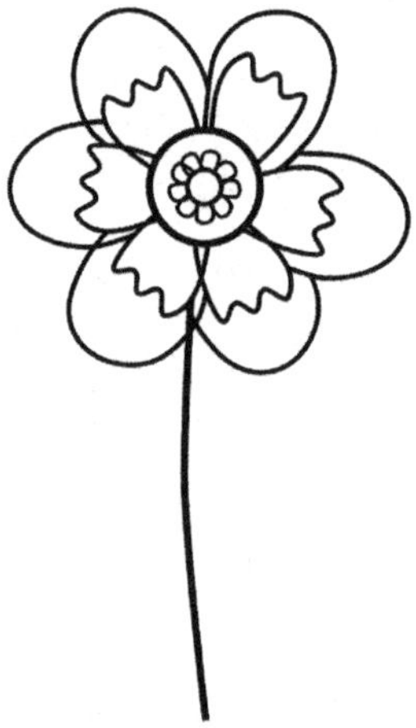

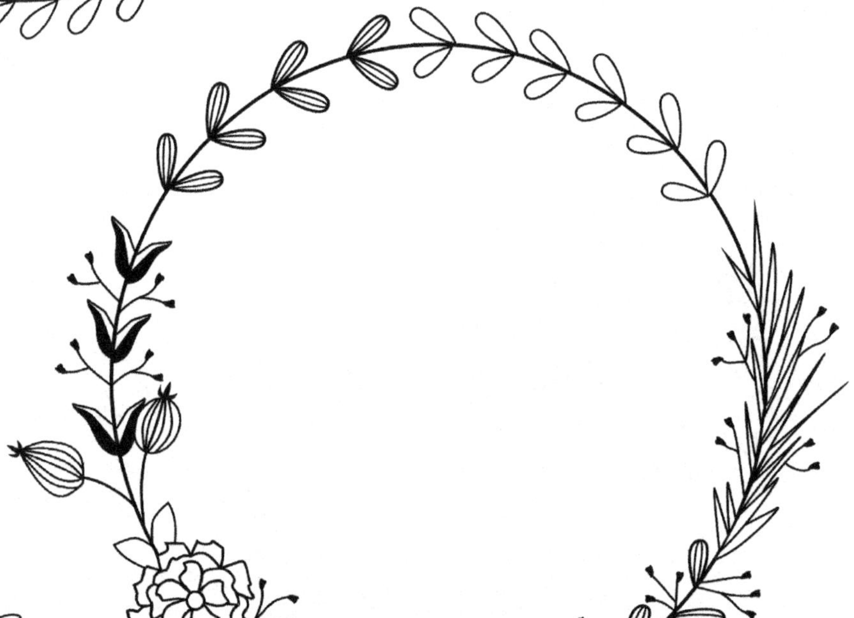

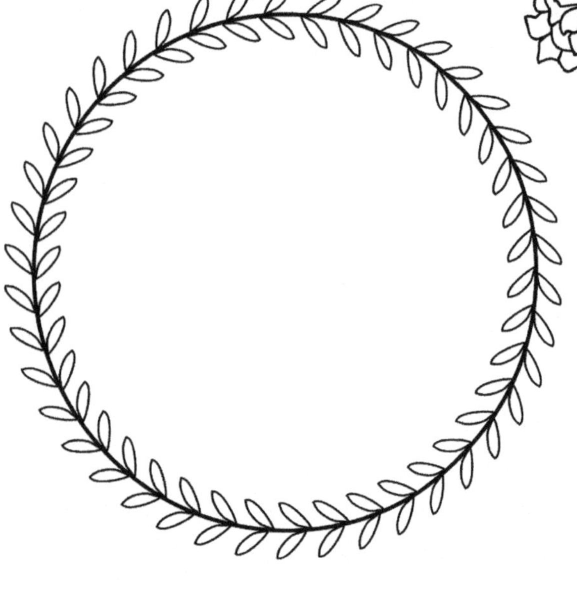

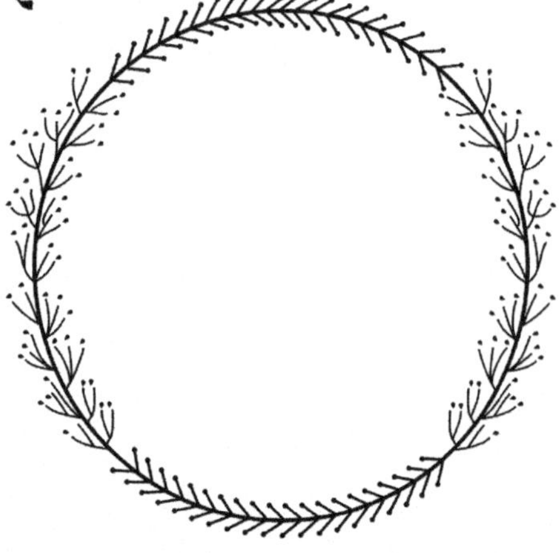

Keep calm and

carry on.

Date:

Date:

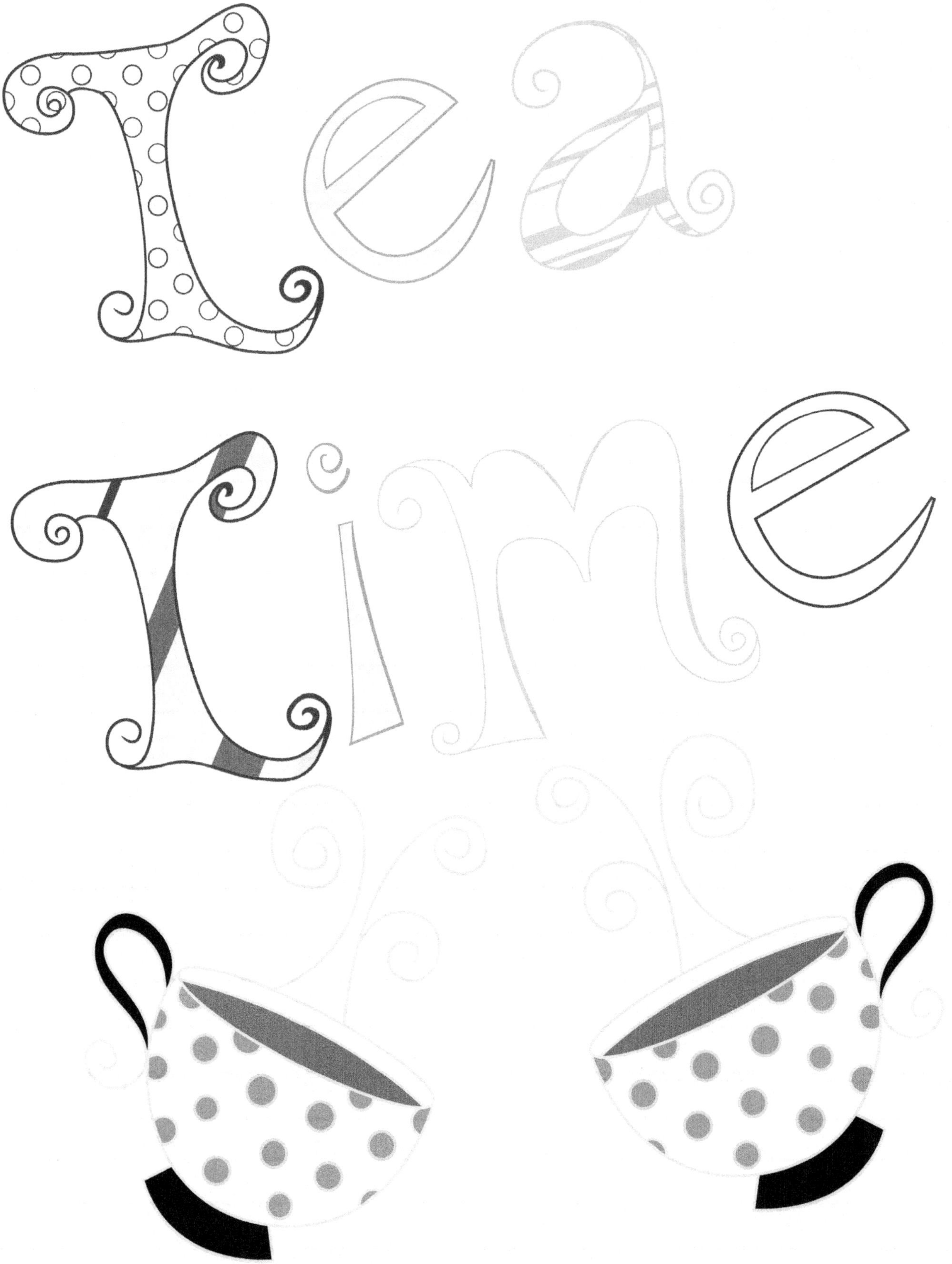
Tea
Time

Date:

You can never
get a
cup of tea
large enough
or a book
long enough
to suit me.
~ C.S. Lewis

Books, Books, Books

Right now I'm reading:

What I want to read next:

Books, Books, Books

Right now I'm reading:

Moments I Want to Remember

Date:

Moments I Want to Remember

Date:

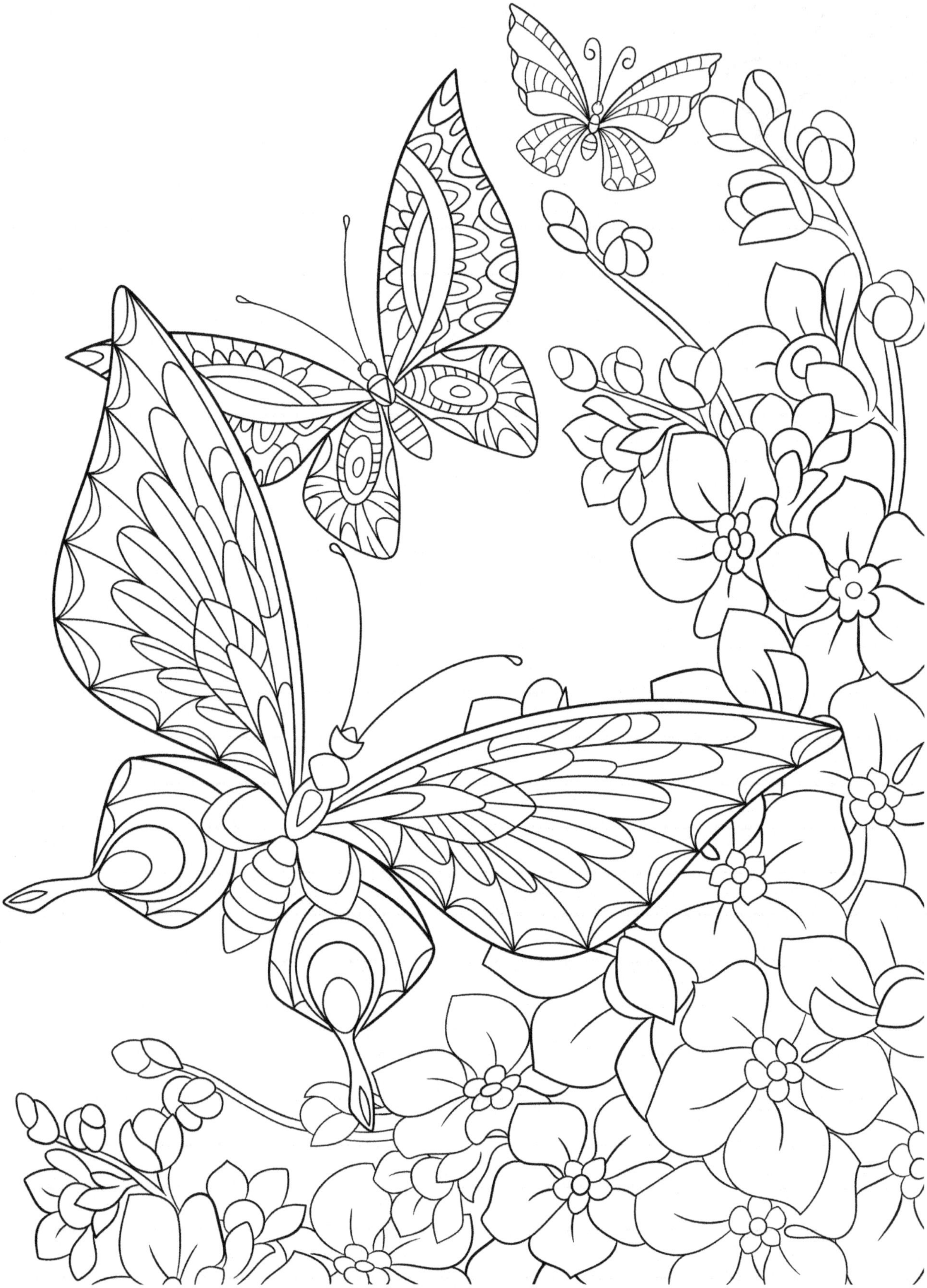

I'm Thankful For:

Date:

I'm Thankful For:

Date:

My Prayer List

Date:

My Prayer List

Date:

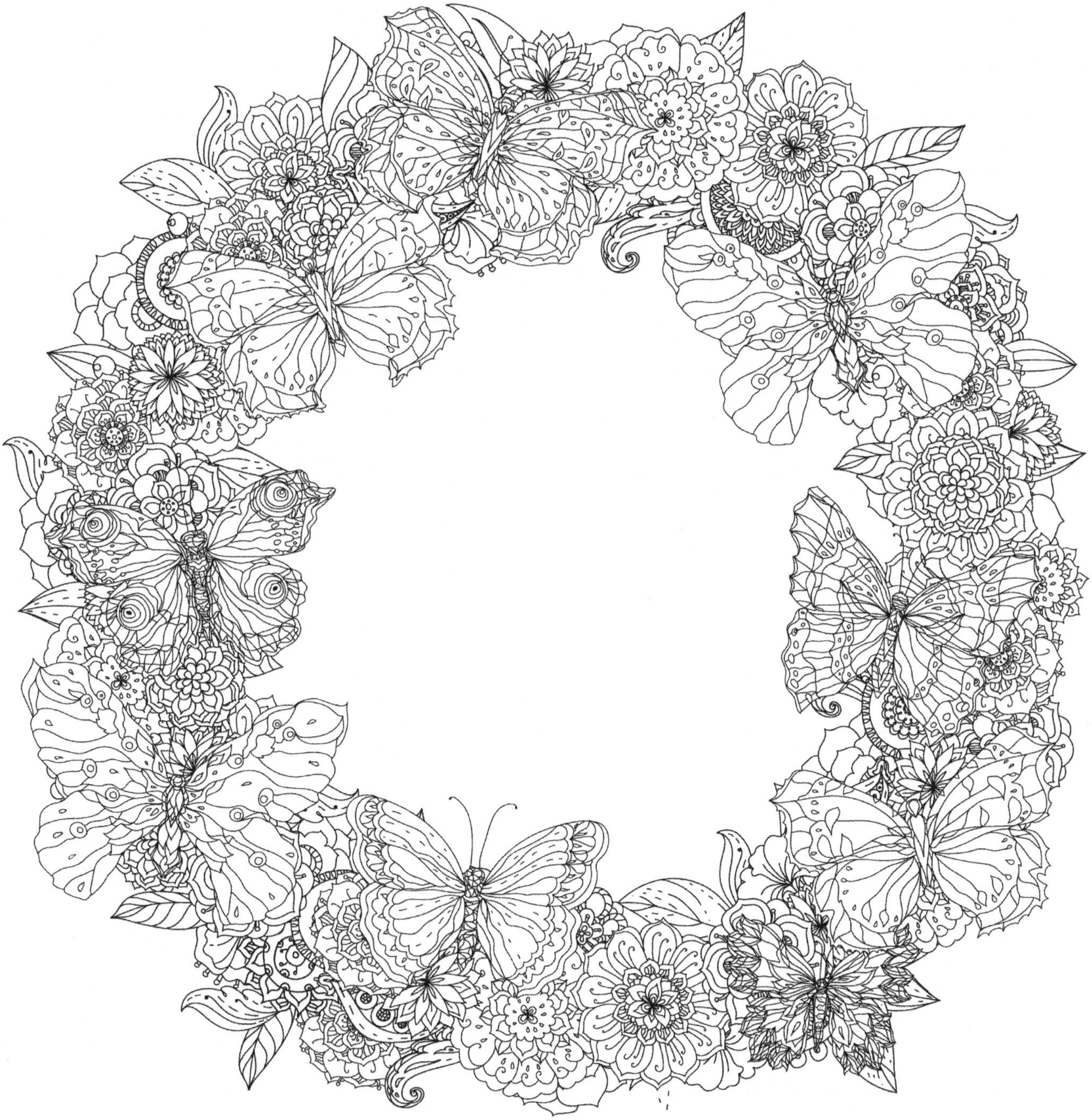

Bible Verses to Memorize:

Bible Verses to Memorize:

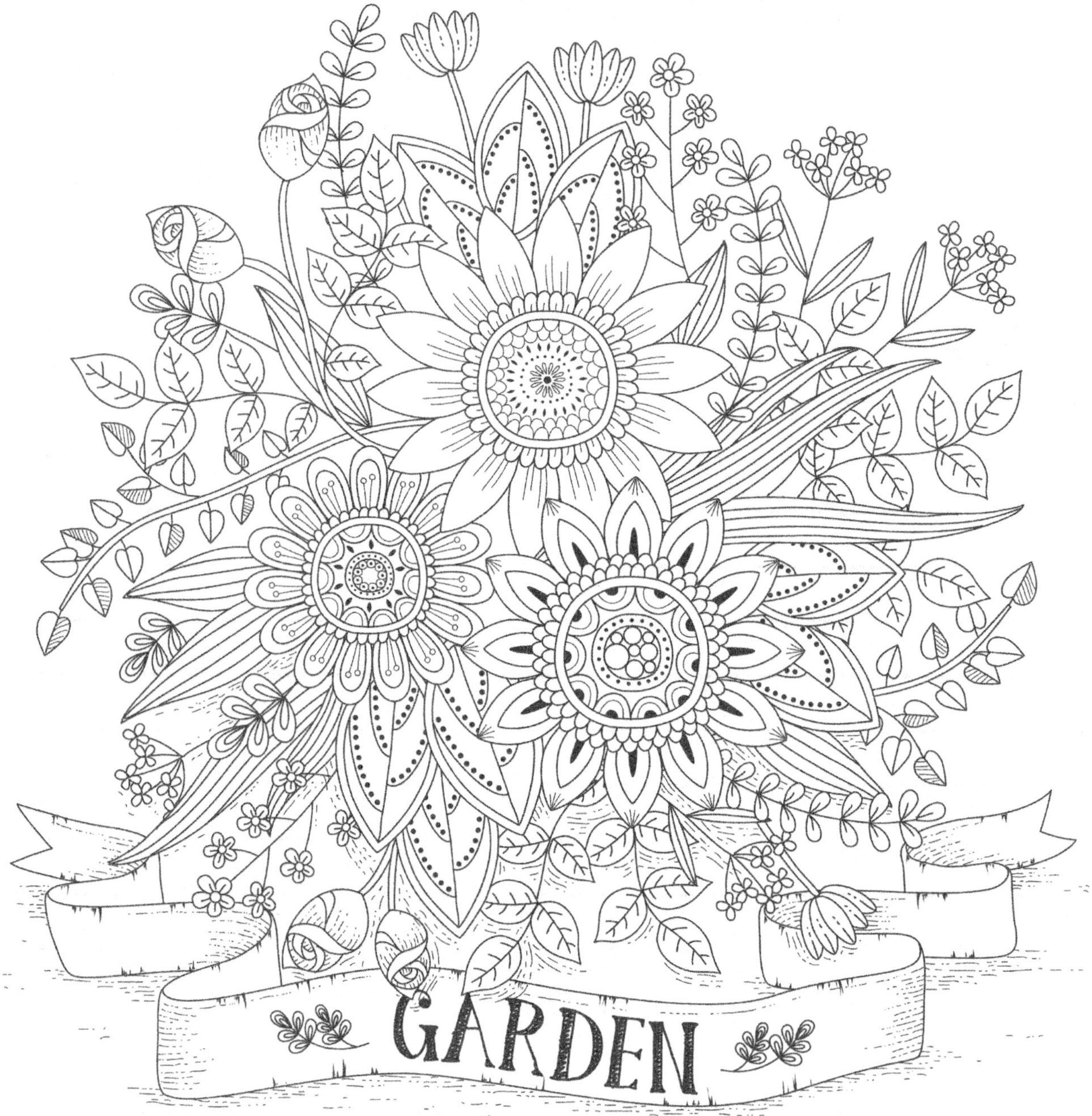
GARDEN

Places to Go:

Projects to Make:

Projects to Make:

Date:

Date:

Date:

Long-term Goals

Date:

Short-term Goals

Favorite Quotes and Inspiring Words to Live By

Favorite Quotes and Inspiring Words to Live By

Fear less, love more.

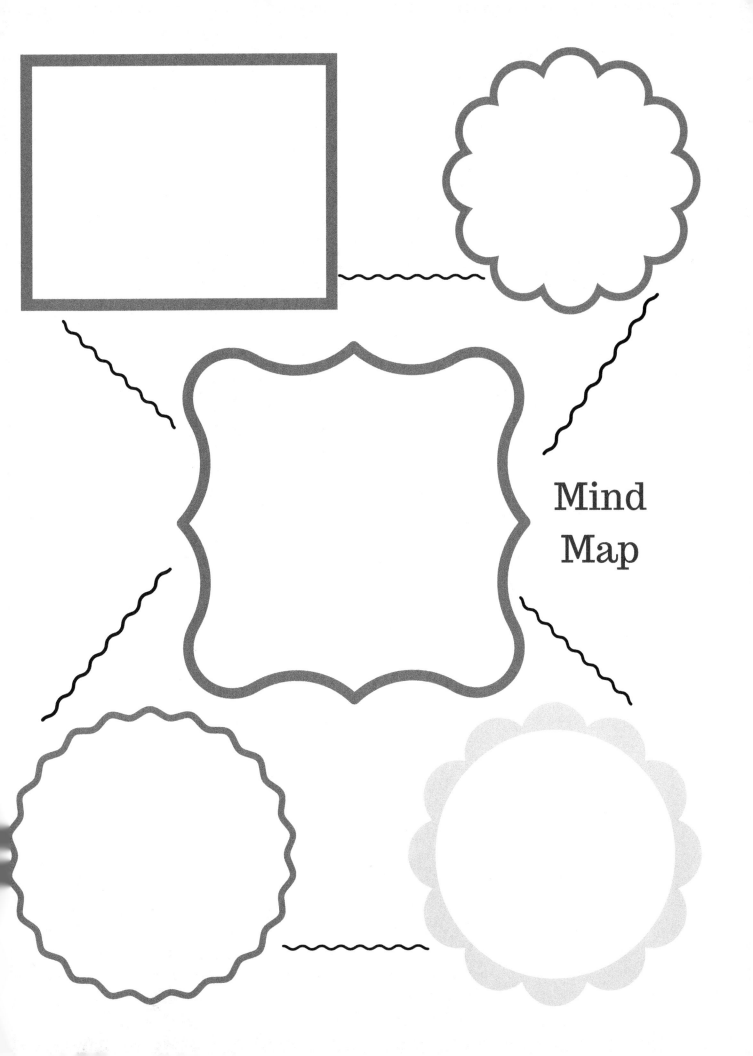

Mind
Map

She believed she could, so she did.

Date:

Date:

Date:

Date:

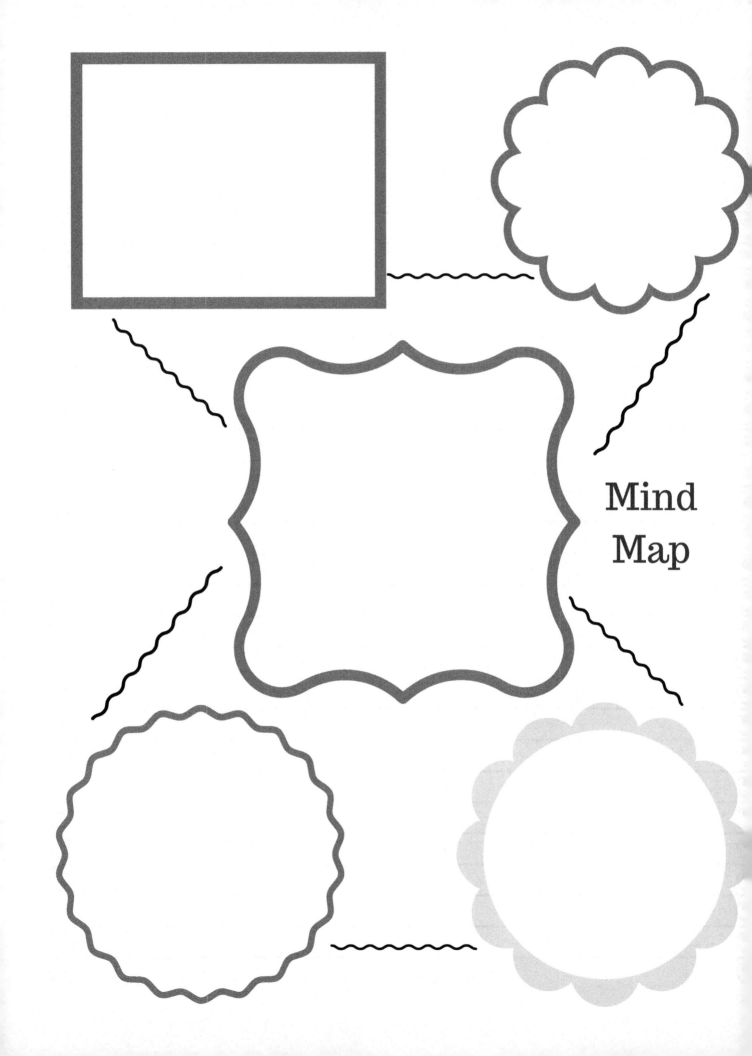

Mind
Map

Date:

Faith

Hope

Love

Joy

Date:

Date:

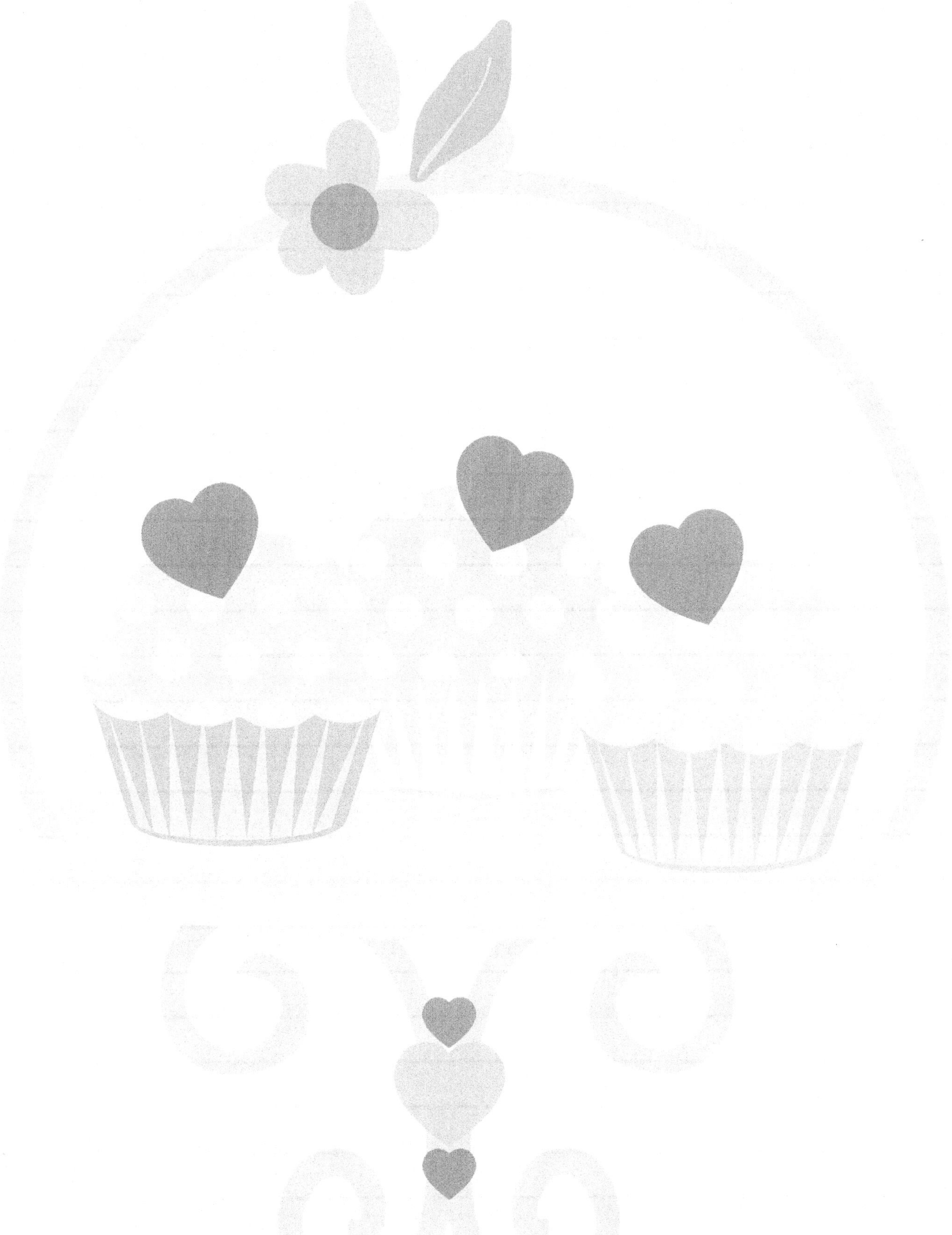

Date:

Date:

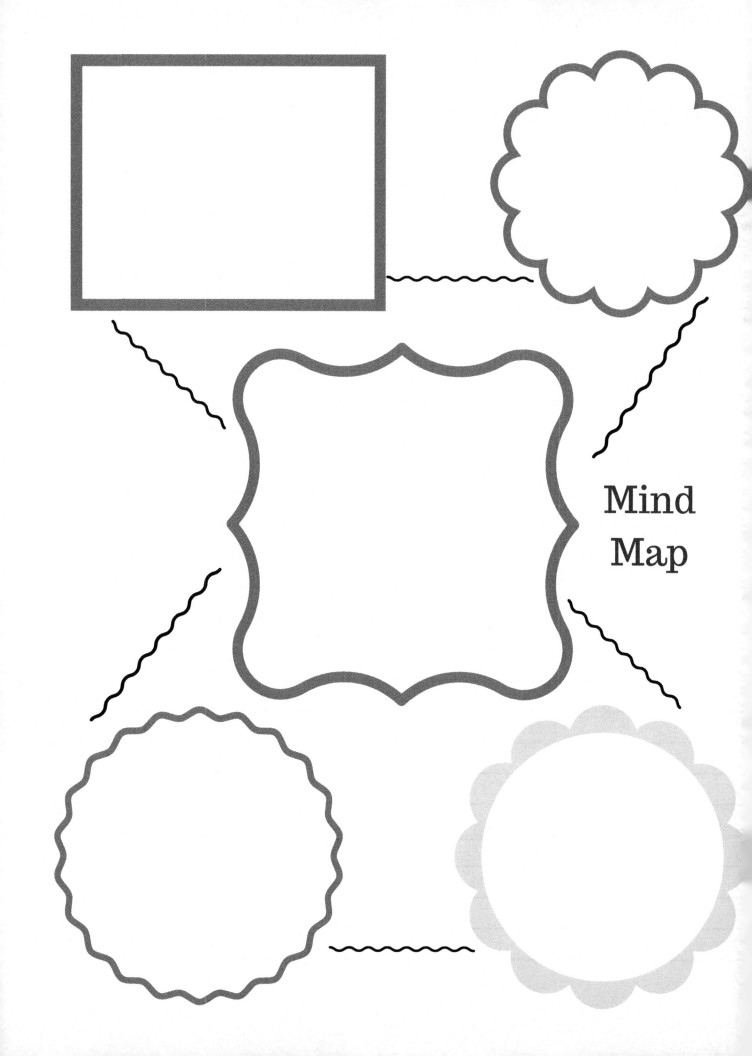

Mind
Map

Date:

Date:

Date:

Date:

Date:

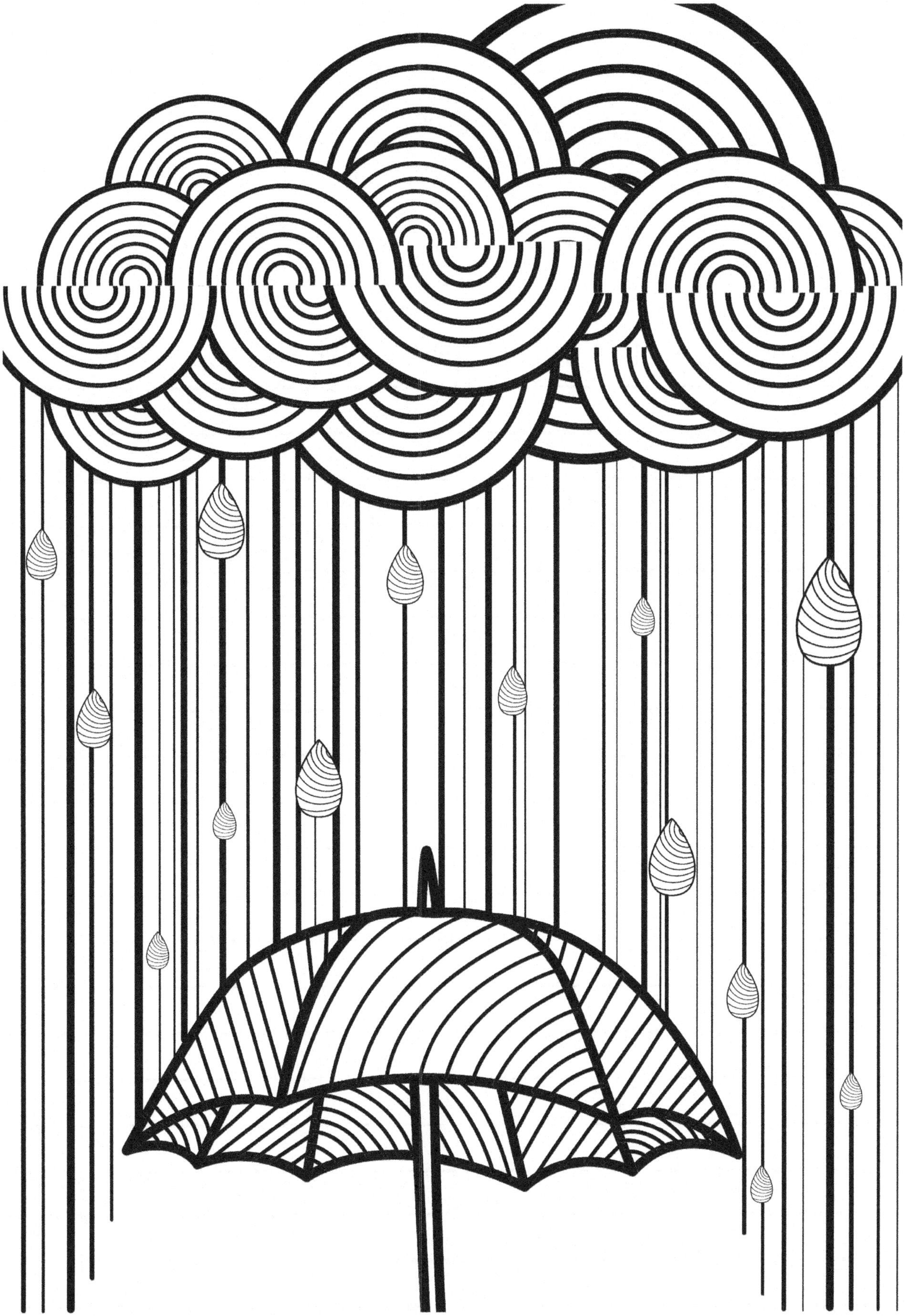

Favorite Quotes and Inspiring Words to Live By

Favorite Quotes and Inspiring Words to Live By

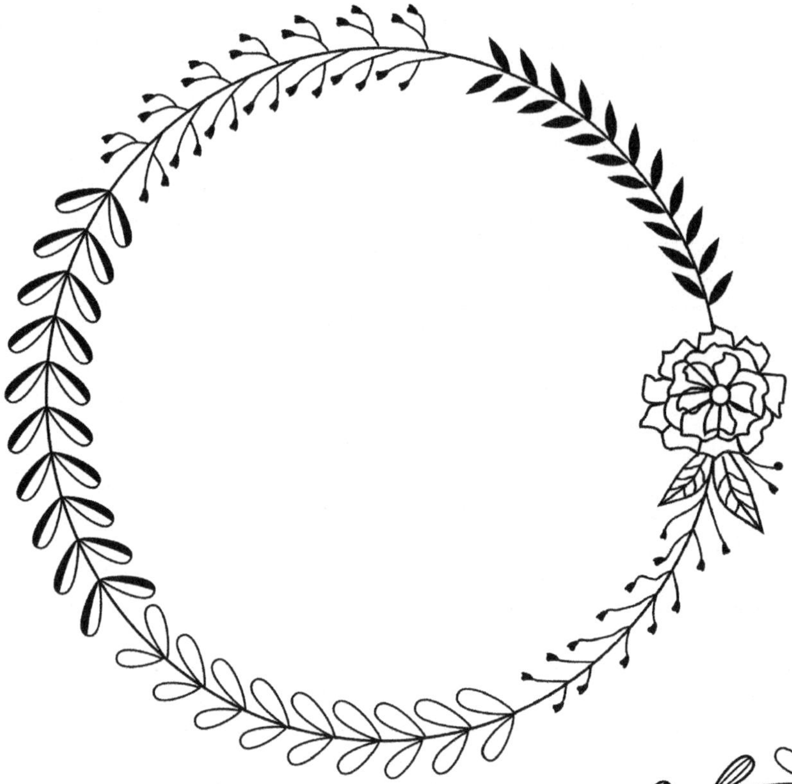
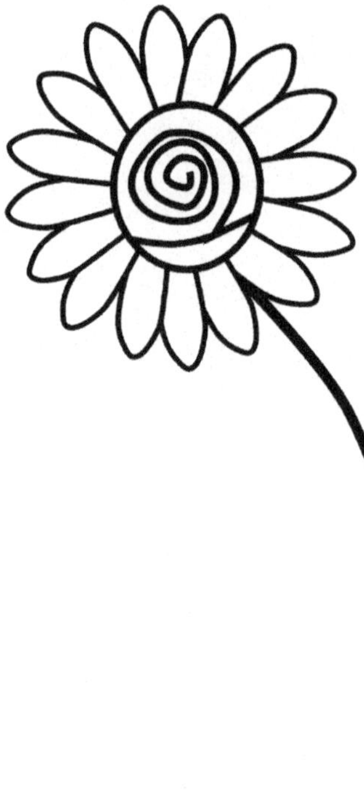
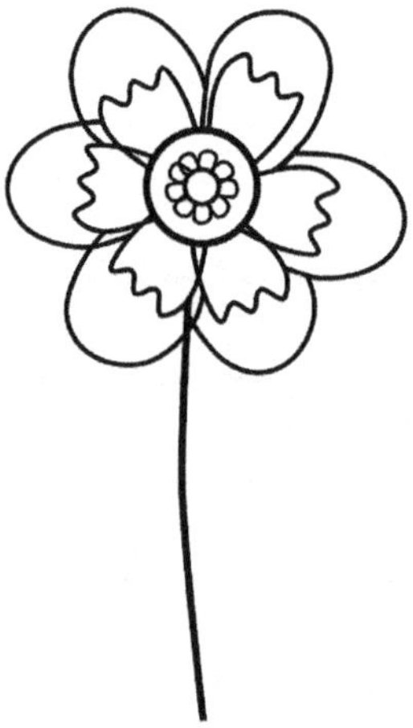
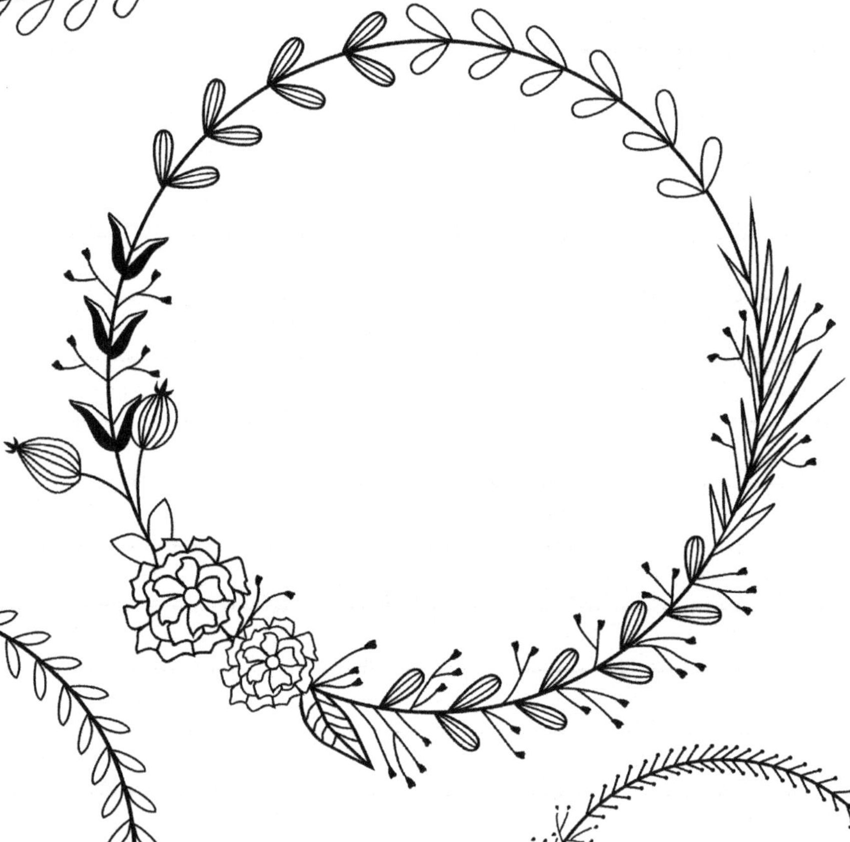
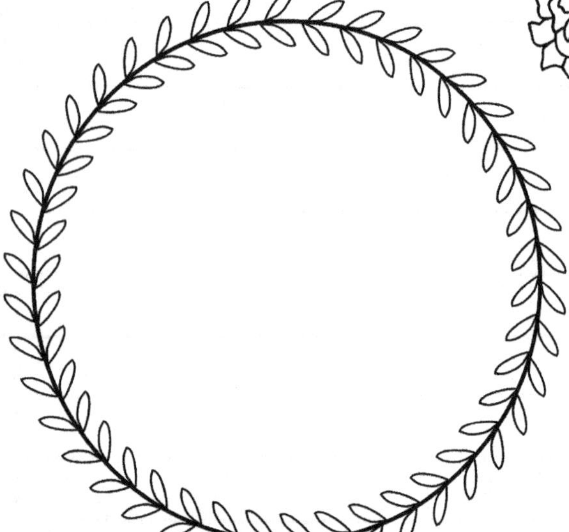
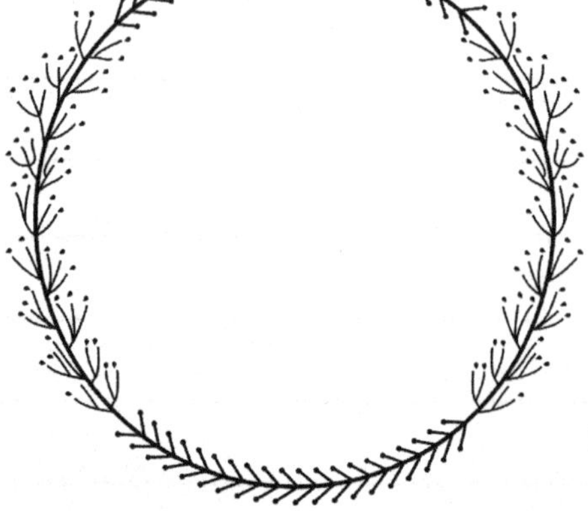

Favorite Quotes and Inspiring Words to Live By

Favorite Quotes and Inspiring Words to Live By

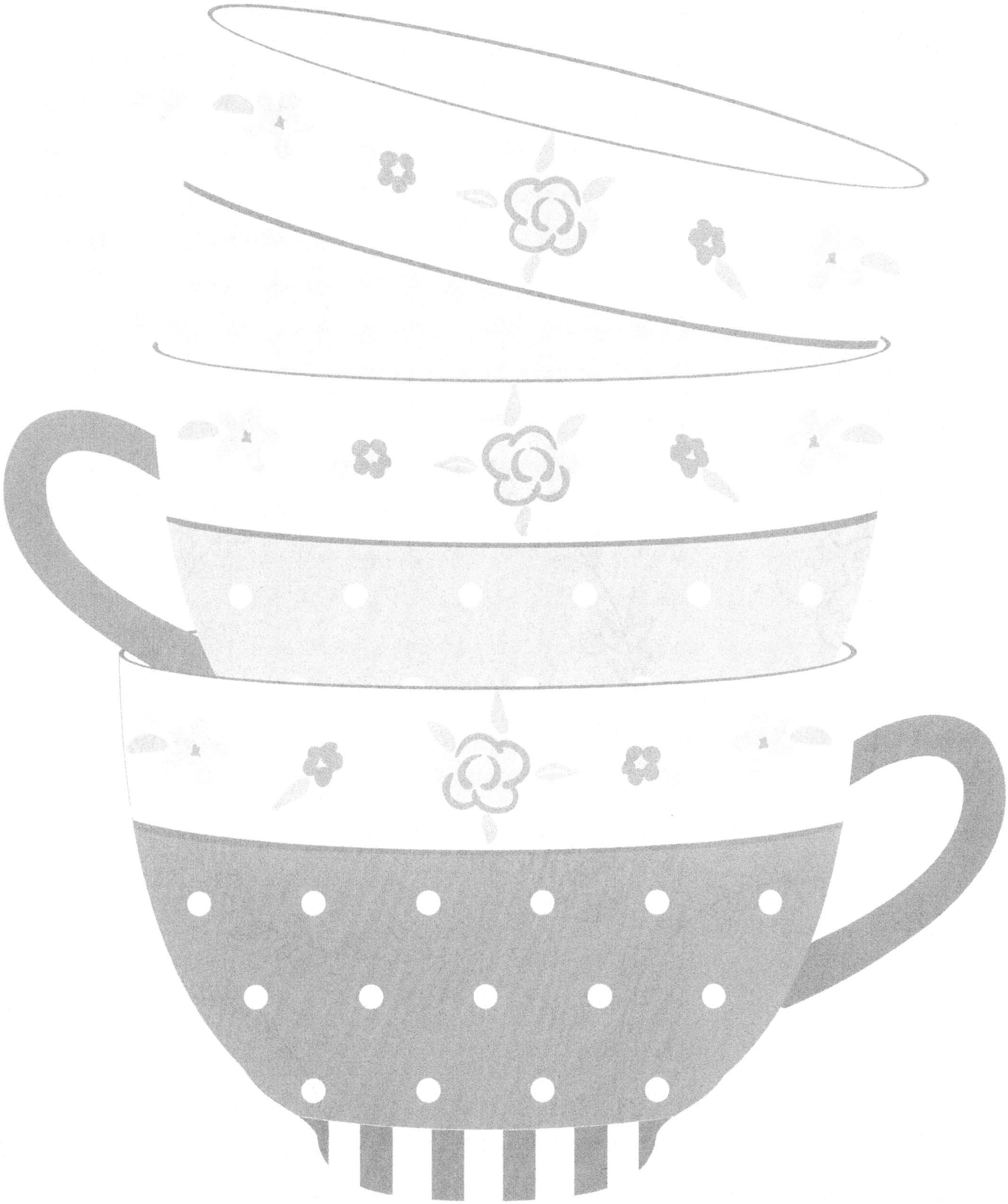

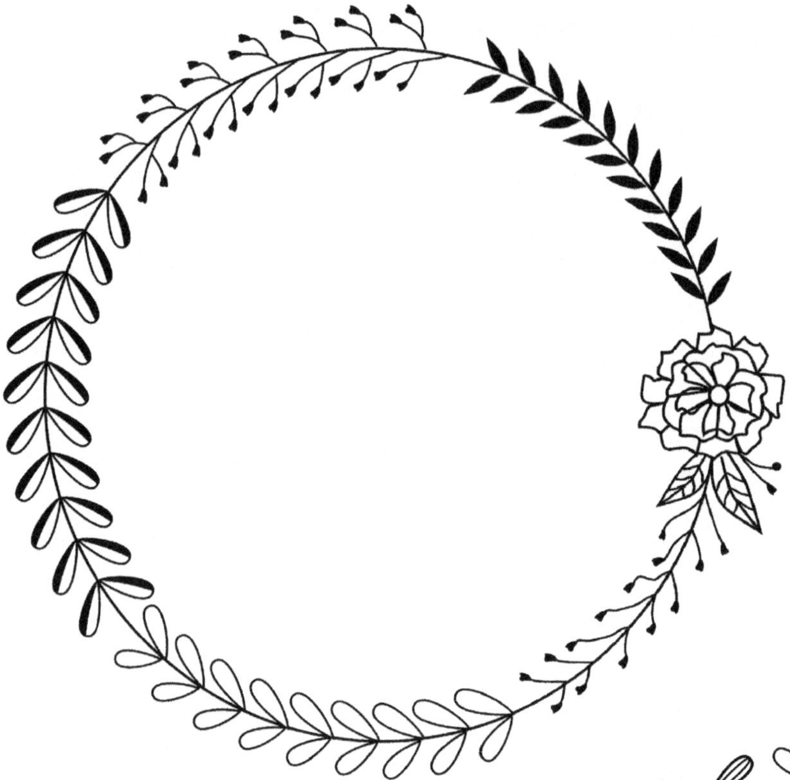

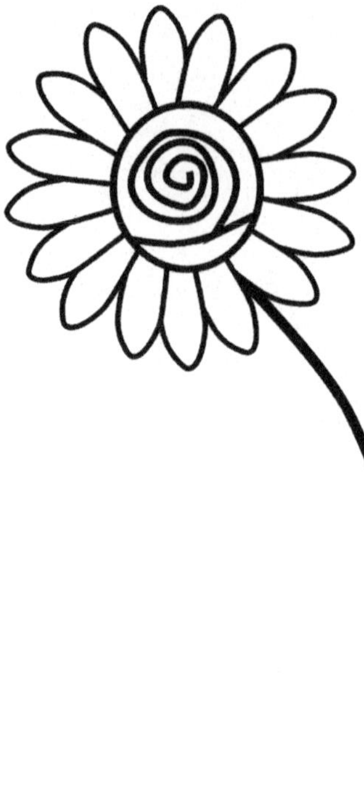

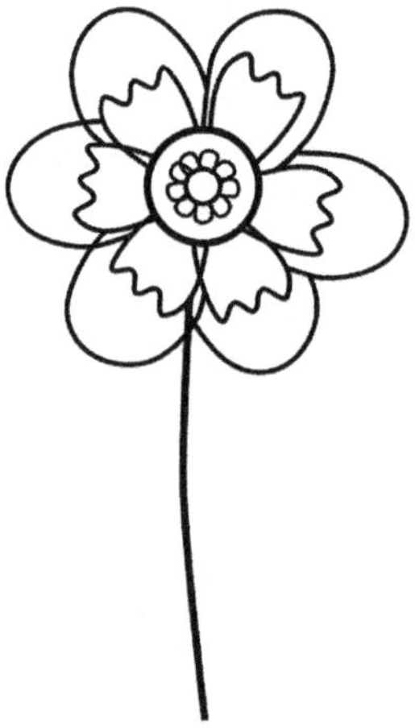

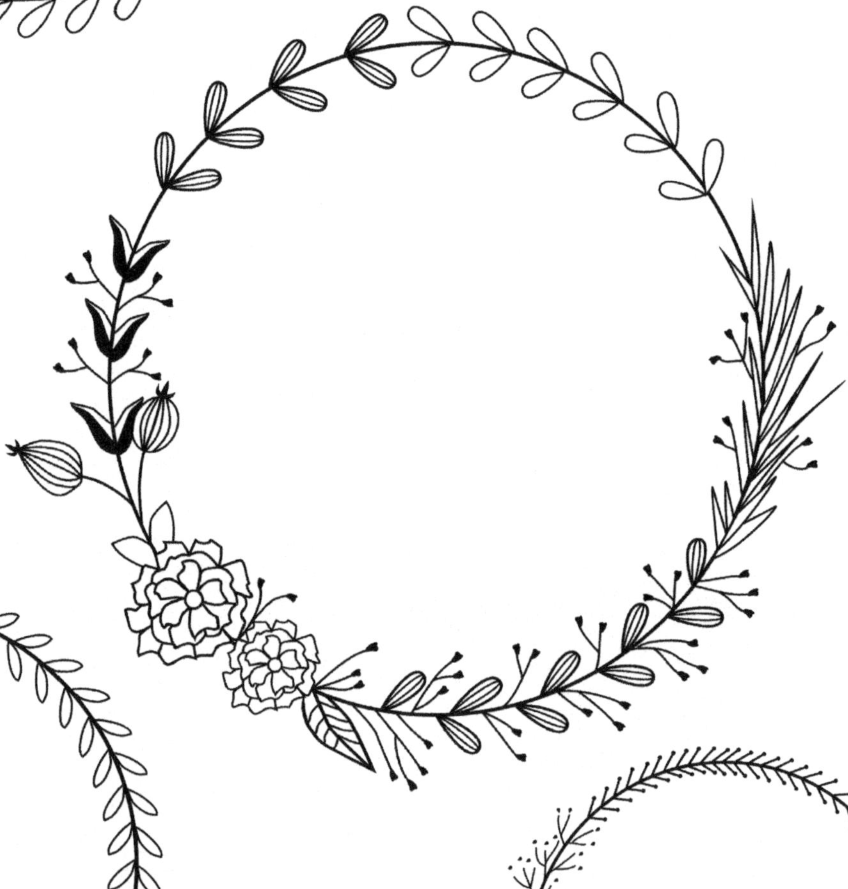

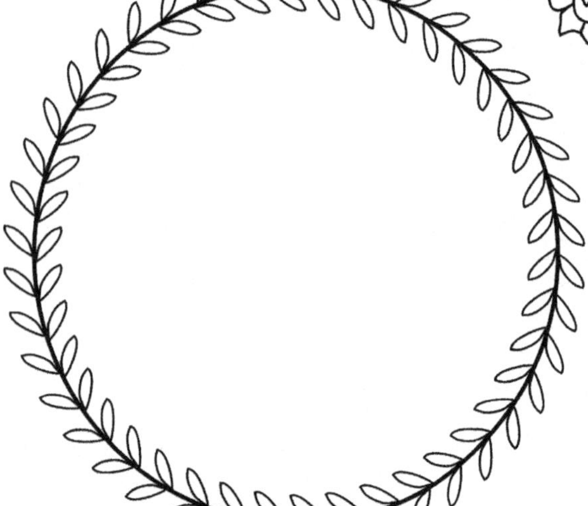

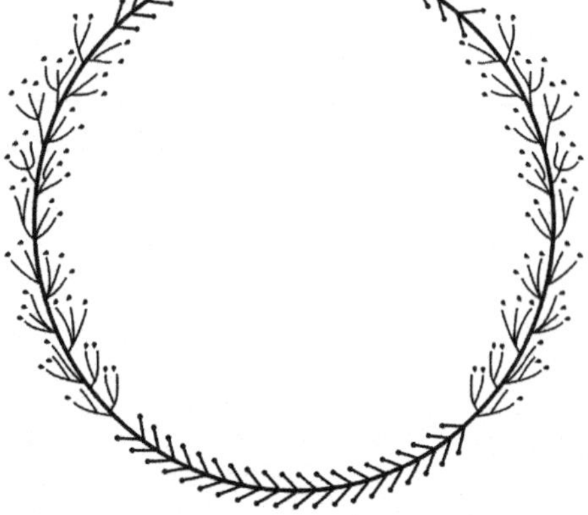

Date:

the future
DEPENDS
on what
you do
today

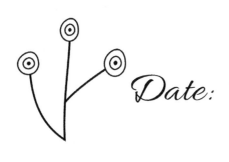

Date:

Date:

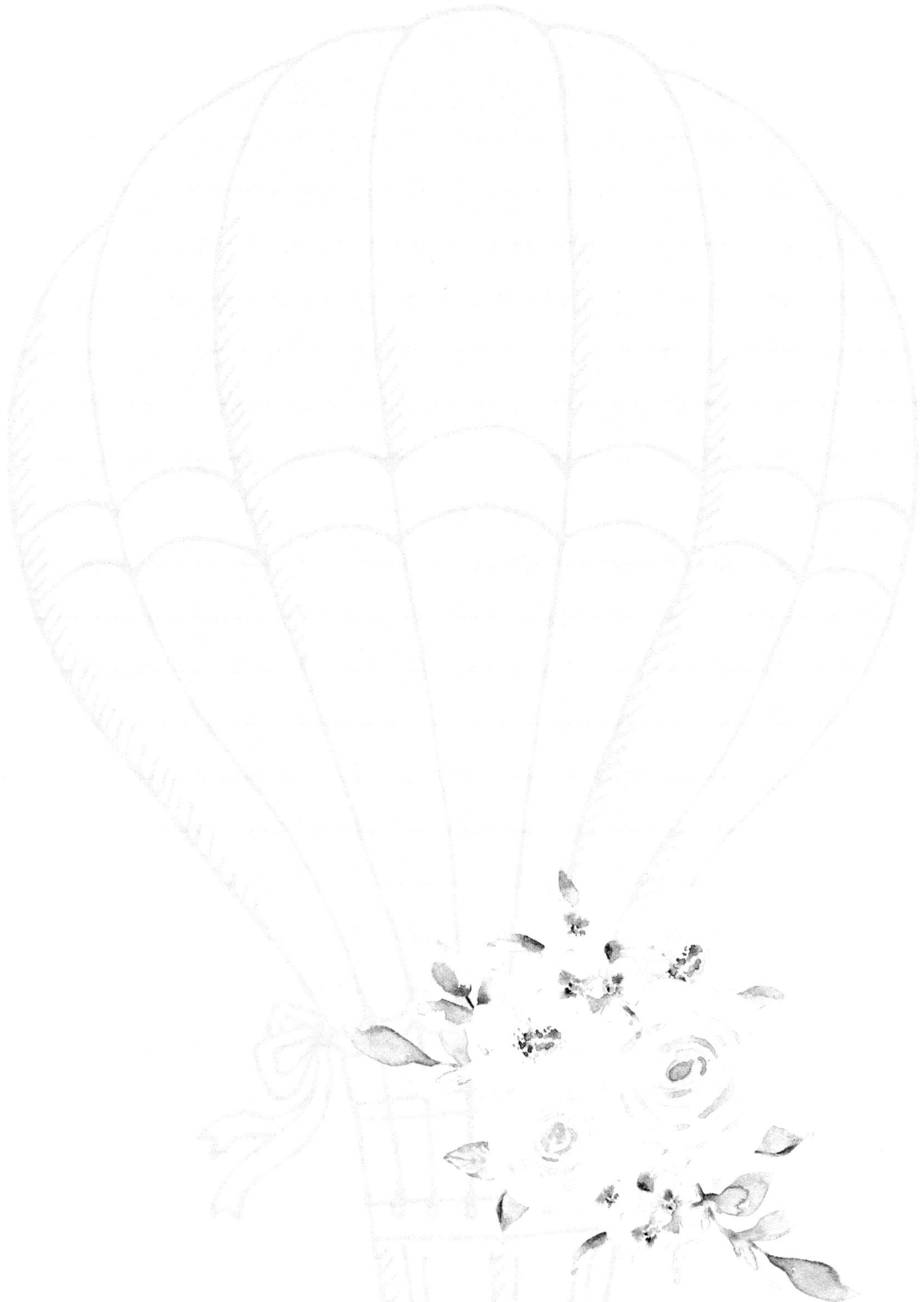

Date:

Date:

Date:

Date:

Date:

Date:

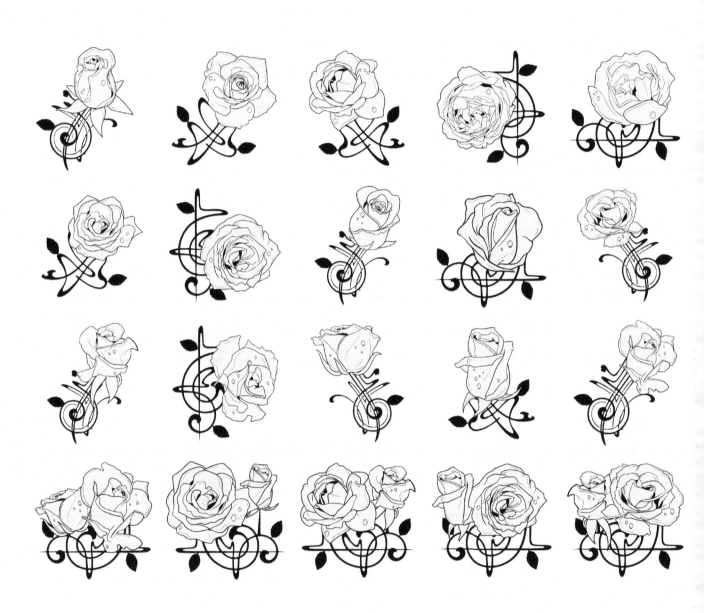

Date:

Date:

Date:

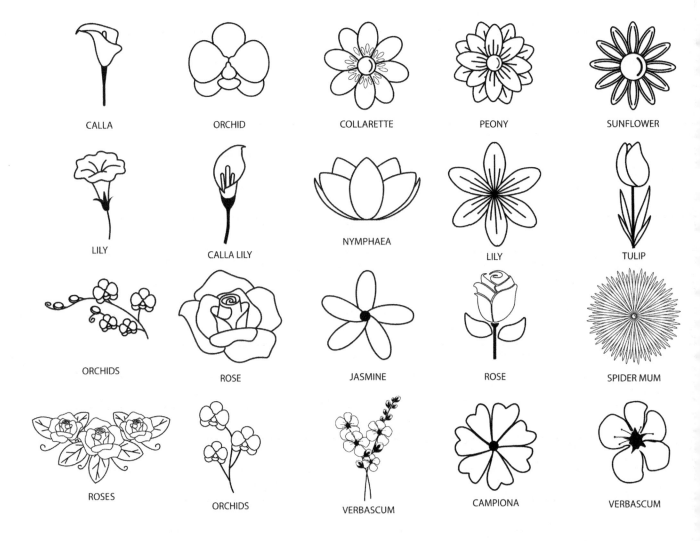

CALLA

ORCHID

COLLARETTE

PEONY

SUNFLOWER

LILY

CALLA LILY

NYMPHAEA

LILY

TULIP

ORCHIDS

ROSE

JASMINE

ROSE

SPIDER MUM

ROSES

ORCHIDS

VERBASCUM

CAMPIONA

VERBASCUM

Favorite Quotes and Inspiring Words to Live By

Favorite Quotes and Inspiring Words to Live By

Cast all your anxiety on Him because He cares for you.

1 Peter 5:7

Favorite Quotes and Inspiring Words to Live By

Favorite Quotes and Inspiring Words to Live By

Thank you for purchasing Mom's Quiet Time Journal with Coloring Pages. I hope you enjoyed it!

Don't forget to look for the other journals and coloring books I've created.

Visit my site at heartandsouljournaling.com for more journaling ideas.

~ *Sara*

Made in the USA
Las Vegas, NV
13 September 2021